CORAL REEFS

Nature's Richest Realm

CORAL REEFS

Nature's Richest Realm

ROGER STEENE

MALLARD PRESS

An imprint of BDD Promotional Book Company, Inc.
666 Fifth Avenue
New York, New York 10113

Dedicated to Jim Tobin of Portland, Oregon

*"What is discovered only serves to shew
that nothing's known to what is yet to know"*
Aesop

Acknowledgements

First and foremost, very special thanks go to Dr Walter A. Starck II. When I was starting with underwater photography I recall being entranced by a series of photos accompanying a story on night diving in *National Geographic*. The techniques and sea secrets revealed were something none of us had seen. That was in 1964 and the author was Dr Walter Starck, a true pioneer of scuba diving and underwater photography.

He built a 150-tonne research vessel and equipped it with state-of-the-art accessories including a wet sub and diving chambers. After extensive field work in the Caribbean, he moved into the Pacific Ocean where he roamed for the next 18 years, visiting, filming, and exploring some of the wildest and most exotic dive locations on the planet. His academic background and practical experience gave him something I believe he shares with few others, a genuine understanding of the marine environment. While some of us feel fortunate to spend a few months a year at sea, Walt did it continuously for over 20 years giving him an unparalleled insight into the workings of the underwater world. He kindly offered to write the introductions and assisted throughout with information, ideas, and long hours of literature research. The concept of this book is his.

I have been fortunate to work with Dr Gerald R. Allen on numerous field trips over the years. Dr Allen is an ichthyologist specializing in the taxonomy of coral reef fishes, and the author of 15 books and numerous scientific articles. His encouragement, help and advice have always been welcome. I thank him also for his considerable input into the book.

Jim Tobin, to whom the book is dedicated, has been a constant source of assistance in obtaining hard-to-get camera equipment and custom made accessories which have enabled me to overcome photographic problems. His good nature and enthusiasm have made him an ideal companion on field trips.

I wish to also thank Phil Alderslade, Mark Allen, Dr Avril Ayling, Dr Tony Ayling, Russell Babcock, Brian Bailey, Baruna Watersports (Bali, Indonesia), Dr Rick Braley, Dr A.J. Bruce, Cairns Underwater Camera Centre, Denise Carlson, Christensen Research Institute (Madang, Papua New Guinea), Jan Clarke, Phil Colman, Ian Croll, Dr Peter Davie, Helmut Debelius, Dr Daphne Fautin, Dr Bill Gladstone, Dr Barry Goldman, Dr Terrence Gosliner, Bruce Hodgson, Dr Douglass Hoese, Anne Hoggett, Helmut Horn, Dr Pat Hutchings, Dr Barry Hutchins, Dr Matthew Jebb, Dr Peter Kuhn, Allison Kuiter, Rudie H. Kuiter, Michael and Jane Lark, Helen Larsen, Dr Denis Lawrance, Dr Jeff Leis, Lizard Island Research Station (Australia), Dr C. Lu, Dr Pat Mather, Mike McCoy, Dr D. Meyer, Elizabeth Moody, Simon Moore, Dr Jack Moyer, Ron Moylan, Roy and Susan O'Connor, Jim O'Doherty, Dr Randy Olson, Peter Parks, Brian Parkinson, Dr John Paxton, Dr John E. Randall, Dan and Gail Reardon, Dr Ross Robertson, Dr Barry Russell, Sao-Wisata Resort (Flores, Indonesia), Smithsonian Tropical Research Institute, Lyle Squire, Janice Starck, Dr Hugh Sweatman, Tatsuo Tanaka Memorial Biological Station (Miyake-jima, Japan), Dr Harry ten Hove, Dr Lyle Vail, Dr J.E. Veron, Dennis Wallace, Paul Watson, Wilhelm P.S., Lois Wilson, and Claus Wolthers.

A CRAWFORD HOUSE PRESS BOOK

Published by MALLARD PRESS
An imprint of BDD Promotional Book Company, Inc.
666 Fifth Avenue
New York, N.Y. 1013

Mallard Press and its accompanying design and logo are trademarks
of BDD Promotional Book Company, Inc.

Copyright © 1990 by Roger Steene

First published in the United States of America in 1990 by The Mallard Press

ISBN 0-792-45459-6

Produced by Crawford House Press
Panorama Avenue
Bathurst NSW 2795 Australia

Published in Australia by
Crawford House Press, 1990
Art Director : Maureen MacKenzie
Jacket design : Em Squared
Typesetting : Deblaere Typesetting

Printed and bound by Toppan Printing Company Ltd, Singapore

10 9 8 7 6 5 4 3 2 1

Contents

Introduction

Coral reefs are very special places. They are the oldest richest natural communities on our planet. In them, that most wondrous and mysterious of all natural phenomena, life, has found its fullest expression. Nowhere else can one find so many diverse creatures living so closely together in such abundance. Complementing and enhancing this extraordinary intensity of life is its exquisite beauty of form, colour, and motion. This is truly nature's richest realm, a fairytale world beyond imagining were it not real.

On a coral reef one can find, all together at the same place and time, living representatives of all the major levels of over a billion years of life's evolution on our planet. The entire spectrum of being is present from blue-green algae and bacteria through all of the numerous types of invertebrate animals to fishes, reptiles, birds, and even mammals with brains larger and more complex than our own (whales and dolphins).

These are vastly ancient communities. Primitive coral reefs existed nearly half a billion years ago, a time predating any evidence of life on land. Though these early reefs were quite different from modern reefs some of the same types of creatures which inhabited them still survive on today's reefs. Many of the genera of present day reef animals are found as fossils dating back to the Eocene epoch some 50 million years ago and some date back to the Cretaceous period or age of dinosaurs about 100 million years ago.

Even today's living reefs often have surprisingly lengthy histories. Central Pacific atolls have reef strata dating back to the Eocene and the northern portion of the Great Barrier Reef began growing in the Miocene epoch about 25 million years ago. The persistence of these communities through vast spans of time with only gradual change underlies their richness. It has afforded a stable environment in which the products of evolution could survive, accumulate and fine tune themselves into the richest, most complex natural systems existing.

A dive on a coral reef is like a trip in a time machine to the world before we humans even existed. If we could somehow go back in time for 10 million years we would find many of the same reefs we have today and their inhabitants would be little different from those we know. Evolution on reefs is a much more gradual process than in less stable environments where adaptation and extinction is mandated more frequently by significant changes in the ecosystem.

In the American tropics we find a unique natural experiment which graphically demonstrates the rate of evolution of coral reef creatures. About 5 million years ago the Central American isthmus arose from the sea, dividing the coral reef area of that region. Since then the separate evolution of populations on either side has produced several hundred geminate or twin species pairs of various reef creatures. After 5 million years the difference amounts to a few scale rows, or fin rays, or spines more or less and slight differences in colouration. Meanwhile our own ancestors evolved through four or more distinct and subsequently extinct species from ape to modern man.

Coral reefs have not only been significantly exempt from natural extinctions but, thus far, human induced ones as well. Despite the popular mythology of primitive man living in harmony with nature, all over the world the appearance of mankind in the geological record coincides with, or is shortly followed by, a wave of extinctions in the native fauna. There is, however, no known instance of human induced extinction of any reef fish or invertebrate. The worldwide total for extinctions of all reef organisms of any type since the advent of mankind stands at one, the Caribbean monk seal. Today's reef fauna still exists in all its primordial richness.

Inaccessibility, large populations scattered over vast geographic areas and the capacity of individuals to produce thousands to millions of offspring have all contributed to the continued survival of reef creatures despite the impacts of man and nature. This, however, does not complete the explanation of the reef community's resilience and tenacity. Part of the explanation lies in the very richness and complexity itself.

The extraordinary diversity of the reef fauna is not simply an effect of stability but is also a cause of it. In reality this is less paradoxical than it might seem. Stability contributes to diversity and vice versa. It begins with the physical environment of reefs. Vast reaches of equatorial ocean buffer reefs from environmental extremes. There are no droughts or floods or extremes of temperature here. Even the ice ages only reduced their geographic margins.

The most dramatic effect of the ice ages as far as reefs were concerned was the changing sea level. Thirty thousand years ago, at the peak of the most recent ice age, the sea level was about 100 metres lower than at present. As recently as 10,000 years ago it was still about 30 metres lower than today and aborigines hunted kangaroos over a coastal plain now occupied by the Great Barrier Reef. The reef community though was still there as a fringing reef at the shore. Reef communities simply followed the changing sea level.

The ability of corals to construct and maintain a stony habitat affording abundant shelter and attachment for other organisms is the keystone of the reef community's richness and stability. Shelter and attachment is a scarce and limiting resource in the sea. Most of the sea floor is a featureless plain of sediments. Rocky outcroppings offering shelter and firm sediment-free attachment are scarce focal points for life. Rocky outcrops, however, cannot follow changing sea levels, grow, or maintain themselves. Corals can.

A fringe of coral around a volcanic island can grow upward at a rate matching the gradual subsidence of the volcanic material back into the plastic crust of the Earth. The result is a reef community maintaining itself for tens of millions of years and in the process creating a coral atoll. A dark volcanic fang capped by over a kilometre of white crystalline aragonite. The ability of reef corals to secrete the billions of tonnes of limestone necessary to create a reef is itself something special. This capacity is dependent upon the intimate physiological relationship of reef building corals and single celled plants called zooxanthellae which live in their tissues.

This relationship between plant and animal, known as symbiosis, utilizes the waste products of animal metabolism, provides the coral with much of its nutrition, and increases its ability to secrete calcium carbonate (limestone) by three to four times.

The dependence of reef corals on plant cells also means they require light. This restricts their growth to a maximum depth of 80 metres or less depending on water clarity. For reasons less clear but probably related to their physiology of limestone secretion, coral reef formation seems to be limited to tempera-tures above a minimum of 18°C. Coral reefs are thus a phenomenon of shallow tropical seas.

Geographically they are generally limited by the tropics of Cancer and Capricorn, 23.5° (1410 nautical miles) on either side of the Equator. However, where warm ocean currents prevail there are isolated reefs at higher latitudes. There are thus coral reefs at Bermuda (32.5° N), Lord Howe Island (31.5° S), and the islands outside Tokyo Bay (34° N).

Within this broad band around the tropical midriff of the planet, reefs are remarkably similar. There are only two major regions of differentiation, the Indo-Pacific and the tropical Atlantic. The former stretches from East Africa and the Red Sea across the Indian and Pacific oceans to the west coast of the Americas. The latter is essentially restricted to the West Indian region and the coast of Brazil. At the eastern extremity of both regions, along the west coast of the Americas and off West Africa, reef development is greatly restricted by cold currents flowing toward the Equator.

The coral reef area of the tropical Atlantic is only a fraction the size of that of the Indo-Pacific. It is characterised by a much reduced fauna with mostly similar genera but different species than the Indo-Pacific and with far fewer of both. To a diver this is not readily apparent. West Indian reefs swarm with the same general type of creatures as do Pacific reefs. Damselfishes, brain corals, cowries, sea whips and myriad other reef dwellers over-whelm the viewer in their profusion. When enumerated how-ever, the figures reveal what is too much for the eye to encom-pass. For example, a rich West Indian reef might have about 35 species of corals, an Indo-Pacific reef over 300. Comparable figures for fishes would be less than 400 and over 1000.

On reefs the colour, movement and conspicuousness of the fishes always captures one's attention. A careful observer of them will notice other interesting comparisons between the two re-gions. Their mass in total for a given area is similar. On Indo-Pacific reefs it is just divided into more kinds with generally fewer and smaller individuals of each. With more species to distinguish, colour patterns tend to be brighter and more contrasting. Overall then, though reefs of both areas present a bewildering kaleido-scope of life, those of the Indo-Pacific are the more dazzling.

Within each region the reef fauna is remarkably similar. On land the distribution of populations of most organisms tend to be constrained by natural barriers. We thus encounter quite different kinds of animals and plants as we move from place to place. Most reef creatures have planktonic larvae. In the early stage of their life they drift freely about in the water. The populations of distant reefs are thus linked by highways of currents.

In the West Indian region where distances between reefs are short the fauna differs little from the Bahamas to Brazil. In the Indo-Pacific the picture is a little more complex. The heartland is the Indo-Australian Archipelago comprised of Indonesia, the Philippines, New Guinea, and tropical Australia, a vast area closely sprinkled with reefs and islands. This is the heartland. Here is found the richest marine fauna in the world.

To the east, across the Pacific distances between reefs increases and the fauna progressively decreases in richness. To the west the fauna is reduced by about a third but remains rather constant across the Indian Ocean. It then increases again in a secondary, but lesser centre of evolution along the East African coast. Here and there is a scattering of locally evolved and restricted endemic species. Such endemics are most frequent at the extreme outposts of the region. The Red Sea, Hawaii, and Easter Island are notable in this respect.

Damselfishes, a ubiquitous and characteristic group of reef fishes illustrate this pattern well. Indonesia has 118 species, New Guinea 103, and the Great Barrier Reef 97. Moving east across the Pacific the Solomon Islands have 98, Vanuatu 78, Fiji 58, Tahiti 30, the Marquesas 19 (of which four are endemic), and Easter Island three (two are endemic). The Hawaiian Islands off by themselves in the North Pacific have 15 species of which seven are endemic. The West Indies have 15 species one of which also occurs in the Indo-Pacific.

Though distance and currents account for much of the geographic distribution of reef creatures their great age brings another factor into effect. This is plate tectonics or continental drift. The idea of continents drifting about over the face of the Earth is, like the idea of evolution, one that not everyone readily accepts. Both concepts, however, are at this point not so much theories as inescapable conclusions supported by a vast and diverse assemblage of facts which are otherwise inexplicable. The mass of evidence and details of the reasoning are well beyond the scope of this book. For the present purposes they are presented as facts. Not dry scientific facts but part of the wondrous reality of our world and our own existence.

About 230 million years ago the first modern types of reef building corals appeared. At that time all of the continents were together in a single land mass we refer to as Pangea. About 180 million years ago Pangea split into two parts. One part, Laurasia, later split again into North America and Eurasia. The other, Gondwanaland, eventually fragmented into South America, Africa, India, Australia, and Antarctica. During most of this period the tropical sea was uninterrupted by land and the Indo-Pacific reef fauna extended right around the globe. Fifty-million-year-old fossils from Europe attest to the presence of many of today's genera of Indo-Pacific reef fishes, corals, and other creatures.

By about 25 million years ago the continents reached positions near their present ones. Only a narrow connection remained between the Indian Ocean and what was to become the Mediterranean. At this time the West Indian fauna began to be more isolated and to diverge into a separate centre of coral reef evolution. About 5 million years ago the Central American isthmus completed the isolation of the tropical Atlantic. A million years ago the recent cycle of ice ages began. The tropical area of the Atlantic was reduced to a refuge in the southern Caribbean and many reef species became extinct. The much larger tropical area of the Indo-Pacific provided a safer retreat with few if any extinctions.

The richness of life on reefs today is a hoard accumulated over a vast span of time and space, brought together by the drift of ocean currents and even continents. This extraordinary richness is in turn inextricably linked with the remarkable stability of reef communities. Self maintaining, buffered by warm seas from climatic extremes and linked by currents over very large areas reefs have afforded optimal conditions for life to survive and explore manifold possibilities. Here, life has focused its attention.

The accumulated richness has in turn shaped the ecology of reef communities in a manner which further enhances their stability. It is currently fashionable to use the adjectives "delicate" and "fragile" in describing coral reefs and their ecology. This, however, is more assumption than observation. Most of our present understanding of ecology comes from the study of relatively simple terrestrial communities. In such communities certain key species and their interrelationships play a critical role. Like links of a chain, if any one is disrupted the whole collapses. Such an idea applied to the myriad species and interrelationships on coral reefs results in an imaginary house of cards; a fragile structure threatened with catastrophe from the slightest interference.

Fortunately reefs are not like that. Complex natural communities are fundamentally different from simple ones. The difference is redundancy. This is not a biological term but one borrowed from the most complex of our own technology, aerospace and computers. Immensely complex systems with large numbers of individually critical components are doomed to failure. Redundancy, that is multiple backups for critical functions, avoids this problem.

On reefs, interrelationships between organisms are not so much a chain as a network of broadly overlapping functions and requirements. A single link breaks a chain. A few webs here and there make little difference to a net. Every function in reef communities is attended by a variety of organisms. No one is indispensable. Absence of, or failure for, one species is an opportunity for others.

The stability of reefs is thus not a static but a very dynamic one. From one reef to another, from year to year or even season to season on the same reef, populations of individual species vary noticeably, yet the community maintains. The important thing is not who does a job but that it gets done. A host of attendants with diverse capabilities to perform each function enables reefs to cope with challenges which would devastate simpler, less flexible communities.

The flexibility of reef communities has had its effect on the evolution of their inhabitants. Under a given set of conditions natural selection tends to favour the specialist who can most effectively cope with those conditions. In the longer term though, conditions tend to change and specialists become extinct. The diversity and flexibility of reef communities presents highly varied and variable conditions. This has favoured creatures who can cope with variety.

Most reef creatures tend to be generalists rather than narrow specialists. They utilise a broad range of food items, cope with a variety of predators, live in varied habitats and are flexible in their behaviour. In short they are opportunists, ready and willing to take advantage of whatever is available.

The behavioural adaptability of reef creatures manifests in many interesting ways. A foreign object dropped on a reef is immediately investigated by the fishes. A sunken ship is colonised by many different reef creatures in an assemblage quite different from nearby coral structures. If food is offered reef fishes readily become tame and even herbivorous species will take meat if it is offered. Conversely, spearfishing makes them wary of divers, more so if a diver has a spear than without it. Nest guarding damselfishes discriminate between dozens of other species. They chase away potential egg predators and ignore harmless species. Following a mass spawning of corals many reef creatures ignore their normal food and mode of feeding to take advantage of the windfall. Butterflyfishes, damselfishes, and other species which normally browse on the bottom swim up into the water column and gorge on the drifting eggs.

Though as a group most reef dwellers may be characterised as generalists, there are among them also quite a few unusual specialists. Two groups of these are especially characteristic of reefs. These are the commensals and mimics. Commensals are creatures who live in close association with another, usually very different, creature. Unlike parasitism the relationship is either mutually beneficial, or, if beneficial to only one, is harmless to the other. Mimics copy the appearance and behaviour of other creatures, often to an uncanny degree of verisimilitude.

Both commensalism and mimicry are highly specialised modes of life in which one creature has totally adapted to another. The ability of reefs to maintain themselves and adjust to fluctuating conditions has resulted in a uniquely persistent assemblage of organisms. Many reef inhabitants have existed for so long that they themselves have effectively become a permanent feature of that environment. This has afforded the opportunity for a surprising number of other reef animals to have adapted to live in some special and close relationship to them.

Everywhere one looks on a reef the larger attached or slow moving forms of life seem to have their commensals. Those that can sting or are otherwise unpalatable are especially favoured. Sponges, corals, sea anemones, feather starfish, starfish, sea urchins, sea cucumbers, oysters, snapping shrimps, and other reef dwellers are all host to tenants living on, in, or with them. Most of these commensals are highly adapted to life with their host and are never found apart from it. The various species of clownfish living among the stinging tentacles of sea anemones are well known examples.

Mimicry is most often encountered among fishes. Frequently poisonous or venomous species are the models for mimicry. The mimic in such cases shares in the immunity from attack enjoyed by the toxic species. One of the most amazing examples though, involves the mimicry of a benign form for sinister purposes. The model is the cleaner wrasse who is itself a commensal which makes its living by removing parasites and cleaning wounds on larger fishes. The host fishes seek out the cleaners and remain motionless permitting the little wrasse to go freely over their bodies and even into their mouths and gills.

The mimic, a blenny, has adopted the body shape, colour, and swimming behaviour of the cleaner wrasse, all of which are very unblenny-like. The disguise is so good that even at close range a diver usually cannot distinguish the fake. Neither can fishes seeking to be cleaned. The fake cleaner approaches a nice tender spot such as the gills or the soft skin at the base of the fins and opening a shark-like mouth equipped with large fangs, bites out a gobbet of flesh. False cleaners are of necessity relatively rare. Their activity makes the host fish so wary of the real cleaners that is is only possible if the hosts seldom encounter the fakes.

The extraordinary diversity of life on coral reefs is paralleled by its teeming abundance. This is especially remarkable considering the generally limited productivity of tropical seas. Primary productivity in the ocean is restricted to about the upper 100 metres or less where light is sufficient for plant growth. In this so-called euphotic zone plant nutrients tend to become depleted limiting production. In temperate seas winter cooling of the surface layers increases their density. This permits mixing and overturn of the euphotic zone with deeper nutrient rich water thus replenishing the nutrients. In the tropics the surface layers of the sea remain warm throughout the year. There is no seasonal mixing and nutrient replenishment so productivity is low.

The teeming life of coral reefs amid relatively impoverished tropical seas is an anomaly. The means by which reefs sustain abundance amid scarcity is another of their species features. Efficiency, importation, and recycling are all employed to sustain the affluence of life on reefs.

The most important element in efficiency of production is the direct coupling of plant and animal tissue. Not only do corals do this with their zooxanthellae but sponges, sea squirts, anemones, gorgonians, and giant clams utilise zooxanthellae as well. This symbiosis or living together of plants and animals permits limiting nutrients to be retained in a closed cycle between the plant cells and the animal host. It also permits the animals to obtain nourishment from the plant cells without having to eat them. Plant tissue replacement is minimised resulting in enhanced food production.

Reefs import food in the form of plankton. A large part of the reef community depends in whole or in part on this source of energy. Plankton feeders includes sponges, many corals, sea pens, sea anemones, bryozoans, tubeworms, feather starfish, and other creatures. Both the clouds of small fishes which hover above reefs and much of the varied blanket of attached animals which cover it are sustained by plankton. A reef presents a wall of mouths to the plankters carried to it in an endless stream by ocean currents. An area of ocean extending hundreds of miles upcurrent may thus supply food to a reef.

Recycling takes several unusual forms on reefs. In addition to microbial breakdown of organic matter through which nutrients are normally returned to the ecosystem there are some surprising shortcuts. The clouds of fishes which hover above reefs shower them with a gentle rain of faeces. Some of the fishes feed on this material. In this way food may pass through several individuals until all possible nutrition is extracted. At the bottom corals also devour it and supply their zooxanthellae with the necessary nitrates and phosphates for plant growth.

Organic debris which escapes the fishes and corals tends to eventually settle out on the sandy floor of the backreef and lagoon. Here it fertilizes a film of microbes and algae which live on the surface of the sand. This in turn becomes a food source for a surprisingly rich fauna which lives on and in the sand. Among them sea cucumbers and burrowing sea urchins are especially prominent. They devour the surface layers of sand along with the detritus, microbes, and algae which are digested out. The surface sand is continually processed in this way at the rate of tonnes per hectare every year.

THE REEF EXPERIENCE

As fascinating as is our growing understanding of the biological nature of coral reefs it is only one aspect of human involvement with them. There is also a practical utilitarian side ranging from rich fisheries to the promise of important new pharmacological substances from reef organisms. Shell collecting and marine aquariums afford many persons absorbing hobbies based on reef life. In terms of value to mankind, however, there is no more important aspect of reefs than the simple direct experience of them.

Coral reefs are life's most awesome creations. They are truly life's cathedrals. They confront one with a potent mixture of exquisite beauty, fascinating history and functioning, profound insights into life, and something even beyond that. That something might best be called spiritual, an ineffable feeling of unity with life. Reefs give us a close-up look at the infinite, the beauty and timelessness of being, and our own inextricable involvement in the whole. This, the reef experience, is what this book is about.

From the air, the surface, underwater, by day and night, through calm and storm, in passes and lagoons, around patch reefs, along the outer dropoff, reefs present endlessly varied perspectives. They are like multifaceted gems with each facet affording a window into a different realm of experience. The photographs in this book are a sample of the views through such windows.

Let us consider for a moment the nature of the actual human experience of being there which is the context for the photographs in this book. From the air a vast panorama is revealed. An endless expanse of indigo sea curving beyond the horizon confronts the reef where a sharp dusky band marks its vertical outer edge. Behind this a zone of parallel turquoise veins denotes the sandy bottomed surge channels of the outer reef crest. Near their inner end the ocean swell breaks endlessly unfurling and dissolving a white curtain of foam across the reef crest. Behind, a broad azure reef flat is mottled with variegated patches of corals. In places currents have swept them into irregular streaks. Turquoise marks where the sandy backreef slope meets a cobalt lagoon. Irregular sharply defined splotches of tans and browns are patch reefs dotting the lagoon.

Even from the sky life is clearly evident. Grazing schools of parrotfishes are visible as tight clusters of elongate ultramarine dots here and there on the reef flat. Several brown ovals on the surface of the lagoon are turtles surfacing for air. A pair of black diamonds near the outer reef edge are manta rays. A hazy multihued aura around several patch reefs is comprised of small plankton-feeding fishes. The elegant white shape of terns seem to skate across the sea as they fly just above it. A pale smoky plume marks a feeding stingray attended by several clearly visible trevally. The unmistakable silhouette of a shark crosses a sandy patch in the backreef.

The whole broad expanse of reef below stretches away narrowing with perspective to become only a band separating ocean from lagoon. At irregular intervals deep passes cut it into segments until in the far distance it disappears into infinity.

If one knows from close-up experience the awesomeness of the outer dropoff, the seething life of the passes, the towering pinnacles of the patch reefs or simply the variety of life living under a single piece of dead plate coral on the reef flat, the whole thing seen at once stretching away as far as the eye can see is an overwhelming experience.

On a calm day a ride across the reef in the bow of a small boat affords a very different perspective. On a magic carpet you skim the surface of an endless blue crystal while a fairytale world flows beneath. Your shadow racing across the sea floor traverses a multitude of wonders. A giant brain is followed by an indigo thicket of stony bushes, a rippled desert furrowed by strange tracks, gently swaying feathery forms of multihued life, a bright blue starfish, a fluted clam big enough for a child's bath and everywhere flitting, hovering, perching, cruising fishes in a staggering variety of size and colour.

At the lagoon the sea floor disappears into the depths leaving a blue void pierced by dancing sunbeams. In a moment coral again abruptly appears. The engine slows and stops. You drift. Intermittently a swell breaking on the distant outer rampart emits a barely audible rumble lending rhythm to the enveloping silence. No rustling leaves, no birds or insects or human activity, nothing but silence and the muted rhythm of the sea. You sit alone in a vast void of empty sea and sky staring down into another world, a world teeming with life. The urge to step out of this one and into that one is irresistible.

Encumbered with heavy scuba gear and sweltering in the sun you take that step off the dive platform at the stern of the boat. It's like stepping through a magic mirror into another world. Instantly heat, glare, and weight disappear. A sparkling curtain of bubbles lifts revealing an enchanted realm. We are on a patch reef, a splotch of coral just beneath the surface of the lagoon. From underwater the coral patch is revealed to be the flat top of a towering pinnacle sprouting up over 30 metres from the lagoon floor.

The reef top is a lumpy bumpy patchwork of various corals forming a cobbled mesa just beneath the sea's level at low tide. A shimmering aura of small plankton-feeding fishes surrounds its outer edge. Magenta fairy basslets predominate. Among them flashing gold denotes another slightly larger species. The vertical sides of the pinnacle are crowded with diverse forms of attached life. Sponges, sea squirts, lacy bryozoans, spiny oysters, sea whips, sea fans, soft corals, anemones, and numerous other organisms sprout from the walls. A jumbled shoulder of larger coral formations surrounds the base of the pinnacle spilling onto the sandy plain of the lagoon floor. Scattered larger fishes can be seen lurking among the coral.

From the air it was a brown dot among many others. From the boat it became a small patch of coral. Now, from the bottom it looms up as a mighty tower, a highrise condominium home for perhaps a thousand different species of reef creatures. Each individual an unlikely and delicate assemblage of matter main-taining and renewing through countless generations in an unbroken chain going back through an unimaginable span of time to some unknown beginning. Each embodies the mystery of life. Each plays a different hand in the complex game of survival. All interact to form a whole. A marine biologist could fruitfully spend a lifetime on this single speck of reef and only scratch the surface of its secrets.

Coral reefs are not only diverse in forms of life but also in their variety of distinctly different habitats. Forests and fields tend to be relatively uniform habitats with one area much the same as another. Reefs in contrast comprise a range of very different habitats in close proximity. Each habitat has its own special sensibility. While diving, your immediate surroundings totally envelop you dominating awareness. Reality is here and now, elsewhere a memory, little considered. Each different habitat takes you in and becomes your world, a world with its own special feeling and realm of experience.

With a diver propulsion vehicle (DPV) it is possible to tour a whole spectrum of such worlds in a single dive. The DPV is a small electrically powered torpedo-like device with handles which a scuba diver can use to effortlessly cruise about underwater. With a DPV we can leave the patch reef and transit right across the reef to its outer edge passing through a range of habitats in a single dive. Like a space probe touring the planets we can pass through weightless space from world to world.

With a squeeze of the trigger we depart. The towering three dimensional world of the patch reef fades into the blue beyond. Verticality ceases to exist and we are in a world of only two dimensions. An endless plain stretches to the limits of visibility.

The lagoon floor is a dusky shadowed carpet of silty sand littered with fragments of coral and shell. As we skim along just above it our turbulence disturbs the finer sediments and we raise a billowing dust cloud behind. In places ranges of 30-centimetre-high volcanic hills arise. A couple even spout a smoke-like plume. These mark the burrows of specialised crustaceans. Elsewhere the surface is pocked by holes of varying sizes hinting at other forms of subterranean life. Tracks and trails begin and end mysteriously. You imagine some troglodyte emerging from the netherworld to attend some nefarious business and disappearing again into the earth.

Occasional starfish and sea cucumbers the size of housecats are passed. A metre-wide crater denotes a stingray's hydraulic mining in search of a meal. Sometimes small fishes dive into burrows and even swim into loose sand at our approach. A field of shepherd's crooks sinks into the sand ahead as a colony of garden eels retreat into their burrows. After a journey of a hundred metres, the plain tilts upward and becomes the sandy backreef slope.

In a minute more we are in the shallows surrounded by patches of coral. Now the sand is clean and white, rippled by wave action which dusts away the finer sediments. Dancing reticulations of light focused by the waves project onto sand and coral. The sombre mood of the lagoon is replaced by brilliance and colour. Gaudy fishes flit among the coral. Giant clams sprawl, jaws agape, exposing opalescent mantles to the sun. We rush on across the reef flat. Several times shoals of grazing parrot and surgeonfishes flush at our approach, their tight clusters exploding into blue fragments.

This is a strange compressed world rhythmically squeezed by the tides. Now at high tide it is all of two metres thick. At ebb the sky will slowly descend onto the corals and the fishes retreat over the reef edge or into tide pools. As we near the seaward side of the reef the sky becomes an undulating silver mirror reflecting fragmented and distorted images of the reef beneath. Our progress also begins to pulse, alternately slowing, then spurting ahead with the swell from the open sea. The coral which had become more sparse in the middle of the reef flat again becomes more profuse. Here however, it is not so large or delicate as it was along the protected leeward side of the reef. It is now small, solid, and knobby, adapted to withstand the battering waves which pummel the exposed outer edge of the reef.

Our journey has taken us to the reef crest where breaking waves crash relentlessly and the reef responds with buttresses against the surging sea. Here the reef grows into parallel ridges projecting seaward. Alternating with and separating the ridges are narrow gully-like surge channels. This structure serves to disperse the massive energy of breaking waves.

We slip into a surge channel and follow it seaward. Its floor is scoured and levelled with a loose layer of white sand and coral rubble. Overhead, the rumpled silver sea surface rears into a peak and curls over as an ocean swell is tripped by the reef. It stumbles and sprawls across the sky leaving behind a billowing curtain of white bubbles which quickly lifts and dissolves into invisibility. In between parrot, surgeon, damsel, butterfly, and other fishes dart and sway in the surging water.

After a journey of some 30 metres the gently sloping surge channel reaches a depth of 10 metres. Here it emerges from between the buttresses onto a fore-reef slope covered with a low thicket of corals. Over the next 30 metres we descend another 10 metres. As the depth increases wave motion decreases and the coral thicket becomes higher, the growth forms more delicate.

Suddenly the bottom disappears at a precipice rimmed by higher lumps of head-forming corals. This is the outer dropoff where the reef meets the open sea in a vertical wall which disappears into a blue-black abyss far below. At the edge there is a definite sense of vertigo. Peering over you experience an instinctive urge to hold back and hang on. After a moment's hesitation, conscious reason overcomes subconscious instinct and we slip over the edge plunging in slow motion into a bottomless blue chasm.

Turning to face the wall we find it covered with a vast variegated tapestry of attached life forms. Diverse, delicate, luxuriant growth surpasses in reality anything imagination might have conjured for Babylon's fabled hanging gardens. Entranced we drift downward letting the tapestry of life unroll before us. Fifty metres down we settle onto a ledge notched into the cliff face like a cornice road of some sunken civilization. Most likely it is a wave cut notch denoting some ice age sea level. In exposed parts it is frosted with snowy white sand fallen from the reef above.

You turn around and face the sea, another tiny reef creature against the massive bulk of the reef. Roving predators patrol the reef face. The sleek supersonic form of a silvertip shark sweeps past gleaming metallically. Far above a squadron of dusky blunt-nosed trevally cruises. In the distance a silver bullet, a tunafish fires through the hemisphere of vision. Below, the unknown beckons toward some invisible limit of survival but reason which led us here impels us to begin our ascent. Looking up, the surface and the sun are clearly visible far away through a blue filter. Silhouettes of coiled sea whips and lacy sea fans sprout from the cliff face. Near the cliff top schools of plankton-feeding fishes form midge swarms of dark dots. Nearby your fellow diver is a larger dot at the bottom of a towering exclamation point of bubbles ascending in a silvery plume to the surface.

Still another facet of the reef experience hides behind the cloak of night. A dive on the reef after dark is very different both in diving itself and in the nature of the reef. You step off the boat and are enveloped in liquid darkness, adrift in a dimensionless void. As your eyes become adapted to the dark however, dim shapes of the reef emerge from the blackness and you notice pale sparkles of light as your movements disturb luminescent plankters. With a wave of the hand you can create a twinkling constellation.

Near the bottom you turn on a bright hand torch. Its beam slashes away the darkness and the reef explodes into a riot of colour. In daylight the filtering effect of seawater and the shadows cast by steep-sided coral formations mute the colours of the reef. At night when you take the source of light down to the reef with you and direct it wherever you wish, the brilliance and contrast of colours is striking. The effect is not unlike that of a stained glass window glowing in the shadowed vastness of some Gothic cathedral, or perhaps a magic cave. Everywhere you point your light treasure of the greatest beauty and finest workmanship is revealed.

The scene in the beam of light is mesmerising. Nothing else exists. There is no sense of depth, of the surface above, or of general surroundings. Awareness is confined to and directed by the beam of light. The reef it reveals has been transformed. Not only the colours but the very creatures themselves are different. Many are different identities. The night shift on the reef is out. Others are familiar daytime inhabitants but playing strange and unexpected roles.

Corals have blossomed with expanded polyps, their translucent tentacles groping the darkened sea for plankton. A colourful, delicate nudibranch the size of a dinner plate has emerged from some hiding place to glide across the reef. Scarlet soldierfishes have left their caves to forage in the water column. Near the bottom iridescent cardinalfishes have done the same. Colourful striped and banded shrimps clamber about the coral on threadlike legs. Elegant auger shells have risen from the sand to furrow its surface in their nightly grazing. Everywhere the lesser creatures of the reef are active, utilising the cover of darkness to venture forth in a predator-filled world.

Tucked away in nooks and crannies the day shift rests. Parrotfishes sleep enveloped in cocoons of transparent mucus they secrete each night. Wrasses bury into loose sand. Damselfishes are hidden in coral crevices. Surgeonfishes, butterflyfishes, fusiliers, and others rest quietly wherever shelter is available. Most have assumed drab mottled nightdress quite out of character with their gaudy daytime hues. Seemingly paralysed by the beam of your torch they permit themselves to be touched and even gently picked up.

At the end of your dive you leave the bottom and ascend into blackness. In midwater there is no sensation of progress and you begin to wonder if you are indeed still going up. A glance at your bubbles reassures you but somehow it seems to be taking a long time to reach the surface. Abruptly you come to a stop, head out of water looking across our galaxy at the Milky Way.

Wherever and however you look at coral reefs, one is confronted with life in dazzling dimensions of time, space, beauty, and mystery. Somehow they also seem to reflect something of the marvel of one's own life and contribute to its richness. Displayed on the following pages are but a sample of the untold treasures to behold in this kingdom of coral castles, the richest in nature.

The photographs in this book are the result of one person's love affair with coral reefs. For over 20 years Roger Steene has spent several months of every year diving and photographing on reefs around the world. His motivation has been neither that of an academic following a career, nor that of a photographer pursuing a livelihood. To capture on film the wonder and beauty he finds on reefs has been his abiding desire. In so doing he has amassed an extraordinary collection of some 40,000 transparencies culled from perhaps five times that many he has taken. Roger operates by his own standards alone. The rejects he discards are often good photos by any normal standards. Invariably when he returns from a diving expedition and has his film processed he is mildly disappointed that somehow his results, no matter how good, do not fully convey the ultimate beauty of the subject. This dissatisfaction then becomes a determination to go back and do the whole thing over again to capture that ultimate elusive nuance.

Roger Steene is, like the reefs he loves, a remarkable phenomenon. For the past 10 years I have had the pleasure of his company aboard my research vessel "El Torito" for a couple of months each year on the Great Barrier Reef and in the Coral Sea. His enthusiasm is infectious and at times, such as at a new diving location on a perfect day, it becomes uncontrollable. This enthusiasm is not limited to reefs. He loves good food, good friends, good times, and life itself. When Roger is aboard everyone seems to catch his disease and enjoy themselves much more than usual.

In many respects he is a quintessential Australian. A larrikin, irreverent, fun loving and scornful of all pretension. The Aussie irreverence and lack of pretension applies to self as well as others. No weakness or failing is too sensitive, no stupidity too embarrassing to be joked about.

Minor disasters due to one's own thoughtlessness get no sympathy from Roger. Instead, they are an object of hilarity. More often than not it's his own disaster such as when he attempted to free up an expensive telephoto lens with a pipe wrench and totally destroyed it.

Another classic example occurred one day on the reef. I was busy on the bottom filming close-ups of small commensal shrimps when I heard Roger's DPV approaching. He zoomed in and circled me as if to remind me of my pedestrian status on the bottom encumbered with motion picture equipment. I looked up and he waved preparatory to zooming off again. This action resulted in the coil cord linking his camera and flash being devoured by the propeller of his DPV. This simultaneously flooded his flash unit, started a leak in his camera housing and wrecked the propeller.

His moment of triumph had in an instant turned into a disaster. Roger streaked for the surface to save his camera, trailing the remaining wreckage by the entangled cord. I was left on the bottom trying to avoid drowning from laughter. When I surfaced a few minutes later he was simultaneously cursing and laughing while trying to sort out the mess.

In between diving trips to exotic locales and gargantuan meals, Roger is a businessman. He has few ties and treasures his freedom. Though he loves women and children and animals he remains a bachelor saddened by the fate of his mates whose obligations prevent them from joining him on a diving trip.

In 1972 I arrived in Cairns on Australia's Great Barrier Reef with "El Torito" from the U.S. via Micronesia and New Guinea. With me was Dr Gerry Allen, his wife Connie and son Tony. While I flew out to Sydney to edit and sell a documentary film I had shot in New Guinea, Gerry and his family remained with the boat. My stay in Sydney stretched into five months. During this time Gerry met Roger Steene and began a close friendship which has endured.

This was Roger's real introduction to the scientific study of reefs. At that time he had his own boat and was already an avid underwater photographer with years of experience. His meeting with Gerry was a turning point. What you photograph is what you see and that depends greatly on understanding. The profusion of life on reefs is also confusing and knowledge of their biology is limited and not readily accessible. Only recently have a few guidebooks and texts started to become available. Scientific knowledge is largely couched in arcane jargon and hidden in obscure journals. Much of what is known is still unpublished. Roger's introduction to the scientific community afforded access to this knowledge.

Since that time most of his diving has been in conjunction with biologists. This particular relationship has proved to be very beneficial to both sides. His indefatigable enthusiasm and good humour are always an invaluable asset to morale and he has made his photographs freely available for use in numerous books and scientific publications. In return he has acquired a breadth of knowledge of reefs far beyond that of other underwater photographers. Many of the photos in this book reflect this knowledge. In addition to the intrinsic beauty of the subject matter, they depict many fascinating relationships and phenomena of life on coral reefs. A number of these have never before been photographed.

His dream for many years has been a high quality book which would in a limited way do justice to the magnificence of coral reefs. He also wanted something much more difficult, a publisher who would let him have his own way with picture selection and layout. This desire was understandable but not very hopeful. Every photographer has seen striking photography reduced to banality through the prejudices and sheer ignorance of the subject matter of picture editors and book designers. Try, though, to find a publisher willing to subordinate their own inhouse expertise in this area. Most dreams however, if focused on clearly enough for long enough become reality. Such is how this book came to be.

Walter A. Starck II
Daintree, Queensland
Australia, 1990.

Environment

Coral reefs are unique among biological environments in that their inhabitants create and maintain major geological features of the Earth itself. They take several different forms related to age and situation. Fringing reefs are geologically young structures encrusting rocky shorelines. Barrier reefs are older, more massive structures separated from the coast by a lagoon of open water usually with depths between three and 50 metres.

Atolls are isolated oceanic reefs of great age rising steeply from abyssal depths. They take the shape of circular or irregular rings of reef enclosing an open lagoon with the only land, if any, being small low coral isles on the reef itself. Atolls are the culmination of a process which begins as a fringing reef around the shore of geologically young volcanic islands such as Hawaii. Over tens of millions of years as the island sinks slowly back into the plastic crust of the Earth the reef growing upward becomes a barrier separated from the shore by a lagoon such as that of Tahiti or Bora Bora. Finally, the original island disappears entirely leaving a coral atoll.

Another major reef type, platform reefs, occur as extensive areas of reef forming a thin veneer on the shallow margins of continents submerged by the rise in sea level accompanying the end of the most recent glacial period about 9000 years ago. The lagoons of barrier reefs and atolls are commonly dotted with still another type of smaller reef called patch reefs. These range in size from only a few to tens of metres across and from low mounds to towering pinnacles forty metres or more in height.

Coral reefs of all types are characterised by a profusion of diverse, exotic and colourful life. They are perhaps the ultimate expression of the phenomenon of life. Nowhere else can one find such an abundance and diversity of creatures so easily observed and accessible at close hand. Here can be seen at one time and place, living representatives of virtually every major type of life form that has evolved on our planet in over a billion years of evolution.

Reefs are not only awesome but they are also stunningly beautiful. Colour, luminous and vibrant in intensity, sharp and contrasting in pattern, dominates the senses. Clear blue sky and cotton wool clouds, indigo sea, snowy breakers, a luminous spectrum of blues mottled by tans, yellows and browns, a distant shore heavily cloaked in green, all on a vast scale. A typical reef scene, itself overwhelming, is only the setting for the close-up view. Here, colour in every gradation of hue, chroma and brightness, using every trick of contrast, complementarity and pattern, dancing with the rhythms of life, ultimately dazzles the eye.

Most reefs, especially oceanic ones remote from coastal influences, possess a feeling of the pure and the perfect. There is no visible dust or dirt, no evidence of death or decay. Only teeming vibrant life in pristine perfection meets the eye. Vast, timeless, colourful, the coral reef environment provides a perfect showcase for life to display its exquisite beauty.

PRIMARY BUILDERS OF THE REEF: CLOSE-UP VIEWS OF HARD CORAL POLYPS; BOTTLEBRUSH, STAR AND BRAIN CORAL.

TURRET CORAL.

A THICKET OF PLATE AND STAGHORN CORALS.   REEF FACE WITH PLANKTON-FEEDING FISHES.

VERTICAL WALL OF A PINNACLE REEF.   THE SHALLOW INSIDE EDGE OF A REEF FLAT.

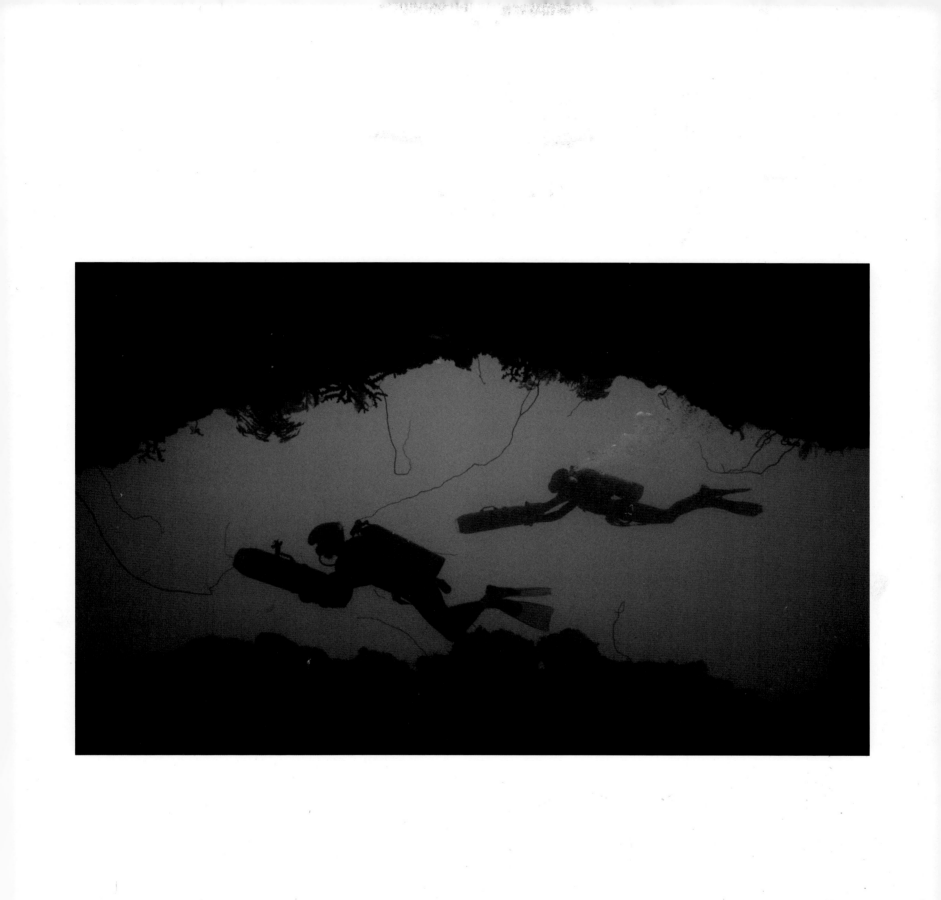

OUTER EDGE WHERE THE REEF PLUNGES INTO THE DEEP SEA. CAVES, GROTTOS AND CREVICES ARE COMMON REEF FEATURES.

SURFACE REFLECTIONS OF CORALS NEAR THE SHORE OF AN ISLAND   LIVE CORALS EXPOSED BY AN UNUSUALLY LOW TIDE.

SAND CAYS ARE FORMED WHERE THE CONFLUENCE OF WAVES AND CURRENTS CREATE MOUNDS EXTENDING ABOVE SEA LEVEL.

NEAR MADANG, PAPUA NEW GUINEA.

ISLAND SHORELINE NEAR MADANG, PAPUA NEW GUINEA.

SAND CAY, DIAMOND ISLAND, CORAL SEA.

A CLASSIC ISLAND LAGOON ENCLOSED BY A CORAL REEF.

GREAT BARRIER REEF WHERE IT MEETS THE CORAL SEA.

Reef Gardens

The garden-like appearance of coral reefs is due to animals not plants. Though firmly fixed to the substrate they are nonetheless animals. They depend on other organisms or plants for nutrition and most have organs such as muscles and stomachs. They also usually have a mobile free-swimming larval stage by which they disperse before settling down to attached life as adults.

From our terrestrial perspective, attached animals are hard to imagine. On land, extremes of temperature and irregular availability of food and water make mobility a universal necessity for animal life. To us land dwellers, animals and motion are virtually synonymous. Only plants are fixed to one spot. In the sea, however, immobile animals firmly rooted to the substrate are common on coral reefs.

Here temperature is buffered, currents carry a flow of nutrition and drought is not even an idea. A wide variety of both primitive as well as some more advanced forms of life have adapted to an attached lifestyle either filtering the water for plankton and organic detritus or subsisting with the aid of symbiotic plant cells living in their own tissues.

The diversity of such creatures is remarkable. Sponges run the gamut from shapeless lumps, bumps and clumps, to fans, tubes and fluted cylinders. They all, however, passively filter the water with little that is recognisable as animal behaviour. Cnidarians (the corals, anemones and their relatives) not only take the form of flowers, mushrooms, bushes and trees, but strange shapes like a human brain, broccoli and lettuce. Their behaviour consists of simple reflexes such as retracting their polyps when touched. More advanced invertebrates such as tube worms, clams, and sea squirts are more recognisably animal with organs such as hearts and kidneys and more complex behaviour, including the instantaneous reflexes we associate with land animals.

In addition to mind-boggling diversity, reef gardens surpass anything on land in delicacy and colour. Supported by water, living tissue can, and does, take the most extravagant and gossamer of forms. Colour, too, has run amok in attached reef creatures. Unlike land plants where bright colours are largely restricted to flowers, in the reef gardens entire organisms are brightly hued with every colour of the spectrum. The end result is a magical fairytale world where the extravagant and bizarre are commonplace.

WHIP GORGONIAN BUSH ON REEF FACE.

BRILLIANT RED CHARACTERIZES THIS UNUSUAL HARP GORGONIAN.

CLOSE-UP OF GORGONIAN POLYPS.

DEEP REEF SOFT CORAL.   MICROSCOPIC VIEW OF SOFT CORAL.

BLACK CORAL SEA WHIP.   MINIATURE GARDEN OF REEF ANIMALS.

GORGONIAN WITH ANEMONES AND BRITTLE STARFISH.

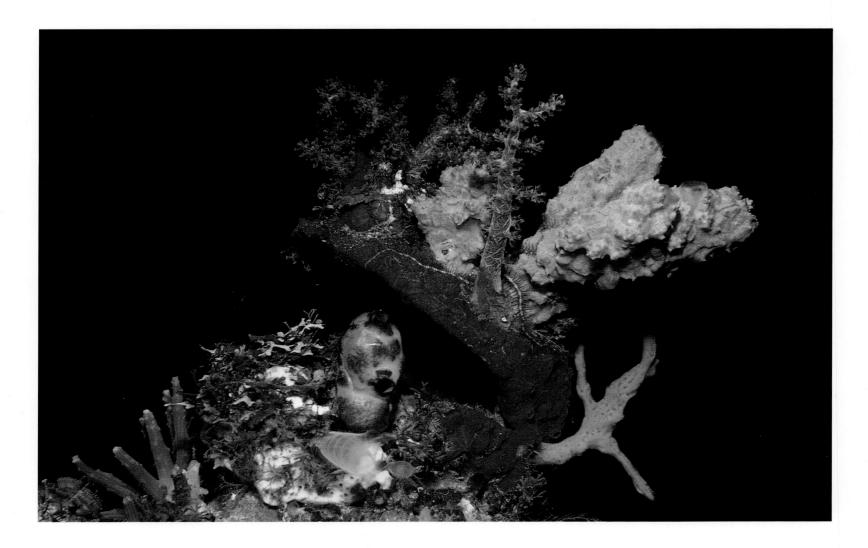

OYSTER SHELL OVERGROWN WITH ATTACHED ORGANISMS.

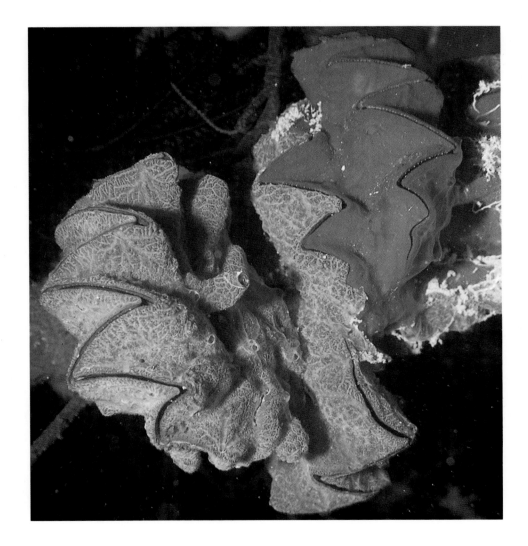

LEAFY OYSTERS WITH ENCRUSTING SPONGES.

AN UNUSUAL SOFT CORAL.

DENDRONEPHTHYA, A TRUE SOFT CORAL.

FEATHER STARFISH SEEK EXPOSED POSITIONS ON THE REEF FOR FEEDING.

BRITTLE STARFISH ON A CRINOID.

A COLONIAL TUBEWORM, POSSIBLY A SPECIES NEW TO SCIENCE.

PLANKTON-FEEDING SEA CUCUMBER WITH EXTENDED TENTACLES.

FEATHER DUSTER WORMS.

TUBEWORMS WITH BURROWS IN A HARD CORAL.

CLOSE-UP OF AN INDIVIDUAL TUBEWORM.

TUNICATES OR SEA SQUIRTS AMONG SPONGES AND ALGAE.

THERE ARE NUMEROUS COLOURS AND SPECIES OF SEA SQUIRTS.

AN INDIVIDUAL TUNICATE.

Inhabitants

Swarming, hovering, creeping, crawling, lurking and hiding amid the attached animals of the reef gardens is an amazing assemblage of free-living inhabitants. Beautiful, grotesque, other-worldly, some are surreal versions of familiar inhabitants of our own gardens, others seem to have materialised from some distant realm of the imagination. Insects and spiders are represented by shrimps and crabs, slugs by colourful nudibranchs and snails by innumerable, beautiful shelled molluscs. Ordinary looking worms burrow in the substrate but others have assumed very un-wormlike, even attractive, guises. Innumerable inhabitants though, have no familiar counterpart unless it be the equivalent of gnomes, fairies, trolls and other such creatures from the depths of our own subconscious.

Beyond the impressionistic experience of the senses and the imagination lies a powerful reality. These creatures are more than just strange and beautiful. They are examples of most major forms of animal life which have evolved in over 700 million years of animal life on Earth. By about 500 million years ago there had developed at least 35 different basic body architectures for animal life. Nine eventually became extinct. The remainder over the succeeding aeons developed innumerable variations on the same basic plans. Today biologists recognise 26 major groups encompassing all animal life. These groups, based on body design, are called phyla. Less than half of them have representatives on land. All are found on coral reefs.

The reef inhabitants span the spectrum of animate being. Sponges occupy a simple vegetative stage of existence with little we can recognise as behaviour. Corals and their relatives exhibit a few simple reflexes like retracting their polyps when touched. Brightly coloured flatworms possess mobility and a rudimentary eye and brain to direct it. Through the more advanced invertebrates, culminating in crustaceans and most molluscs, there is a general pattern of increasingly sophisticated mobility, sensory systems, and a brain to co-ordinate movement and process sensory input. Up to this point we find behaviour is largely fixed and instinctive with minimal ability to learn.

At the next level of evolution, that of fishes and the highest invertebrates, squids and octopi, we find this trend in evolution has reached a threshold whereby stored information from individual experience, i.e. learning, has become an important aspect of behaviour. With it comes the individual differences we call personality. Finally, there are the cetaceans, the whales and dolphins with brains larger and more complex than our own. Their intelligence is obvious. Its concerns and capacities are beyond our present understanding.

Beautiful or grotesque, familiar yet strange, ephemeral but timeless, simple and mysterious, the reef inhabitants embody the essential wonder of life itself. Delicate unlikely assemblages of matter persisting over unimaginable spans of time. Tiny bits of the cosmos interacting with the whole from the molecules around their bodies to the influence of sun and moon to the random genetic changes induced by radiation coming from the infinite reaches of space and time.

A NOCTURNAL REEF PROWLER, THE HINGEBEAK SHRIMP.

ANOTHER HINGEBEAK SHRIMP. THIS SPECIES LIVES IN GROUPS.

MANTIS SHRIMPS ARE THE REEF EQUIVALENT OF THE PREYING MANTIS.   A FINGERNAIL SIZE SHRIMP USUALLY ASSOCIATED WITH ANEMONES.

THE BUMBLEBEE SHRIMP, ANOTHER TINY COLOURFUL CRUSTACEAN.

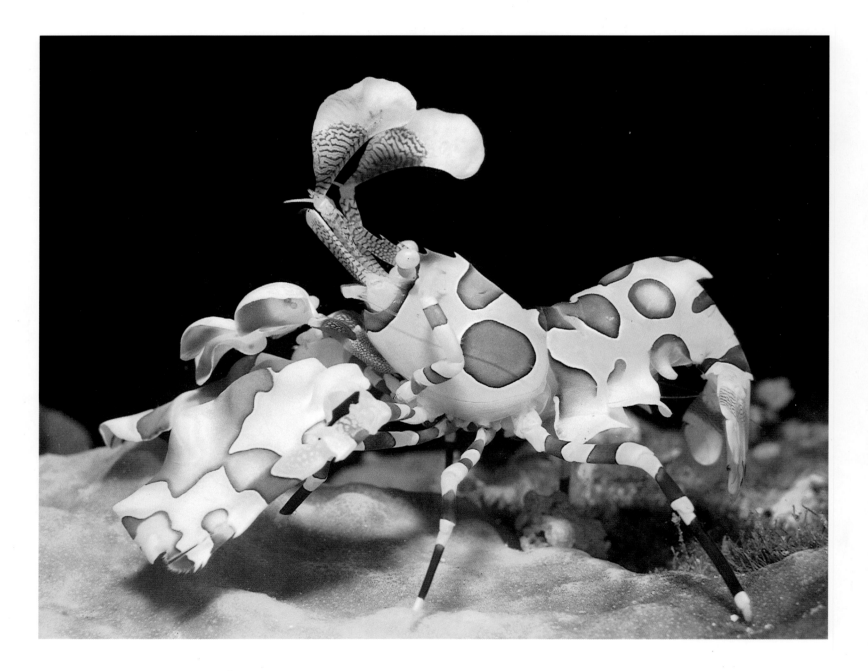

THE UNIQUE AND SPECTACULAR HARLEQUIN SHRIMP.

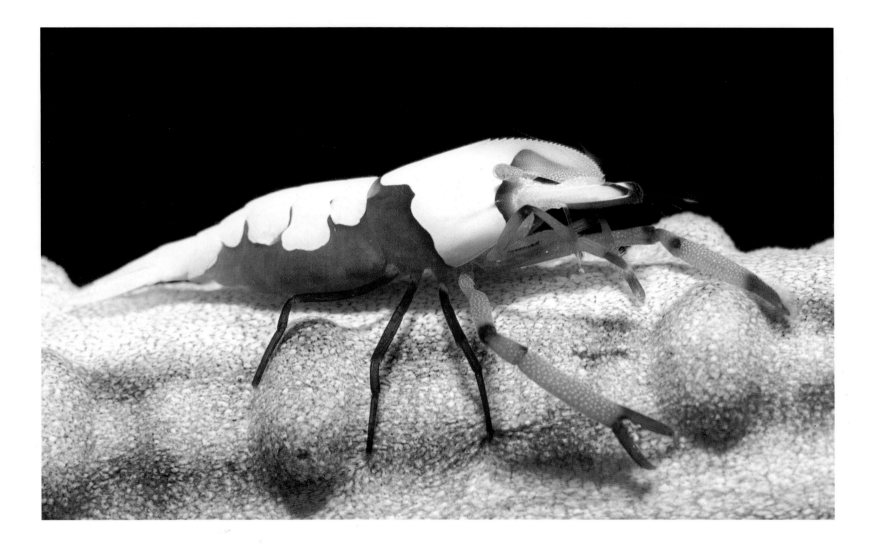

IMPERIAL SHRIMP ON SYNAPTID HOLOTHURIAN.

THE SQUAT LOBSTER, A DISTANT RELATIVE OF HERMIT CRABS.

SKELETON SHRIMPS ON A HYDROID.

THE ZEBRA WORM. ON REEFS, EVEN WORMS CAN BE COLOURFUL.

A PAIR OF PIPEFISHES ON AN ENCRUSTING SPONGE.

A COMMON TALPA COWRIE.

THE RARE AND VALUABLE BRINDLED COWRIE.

THE ASS'S EAR, A TROPICAL ABALONE.

A COLOURFUL REEF SNAIL, THE BUBBLE SHELL.

NUDIBRANCHS AND SEA SLUGS ARE MARINE SNAILS WITHOUT SHELLS.   LEAFY SAP SLUG.

WESTERN AUSTRALIAN DORID.

THEY COME IN A VARIETY OF SPECTACULAR SHAPES AND COLOURS.   GREENSPOT DORID.

LETTUCE LEAF SLUG.   PURPLE STRIPED DORID.

CREATURE FROM INNERSPACE, A REEF SQUID.

THE CHAMBERED NAUTILUS, TIME TRAVELLER FROM THE DISTANT PAST.

THE GROUPERS ARE THE FRIENDLY GIANTS OF THE REEF.

AN UNUSUAL SCORPIONFISH RELATIVE.   THE COWFISH HAS A RIGID EXTERNAL ARMOUR OF INTERLOCKED HEXAGONAL SCALES.

Plankton

Plankton, the living soup of creatures who live suspended and drifting with the water, plays a vital role in the biology of coral reefs. Like cities, reefs must import food to sustain their dense populations. Feeding on plankton drifting past enables reef creatures to harvest the produce of an area of the sea many times larger than the reef itself. Virtually all of the attached reef animals depend in whole or in part on plankton for sustenance as do the clouds of plankton-feeding fishes that swarm above reefs.

Plankton includes a host of diverse organisms ranging from microscopic single-celled bacteria, yeasts, fungi, algae, and protozoans through millimetre to centimetre-sized crustaceans, arrow worms, salps and numerous other creatures, to jellyfishes a half-metre in diameter. At the planktonic extreme one colonial salp of temperate waters grows to over 20 metres in length and two metres or more in diameter.

In addition to creatures that spend their entire lives drifting, plankton includes the eggs, larvae and juveniles of both free-swimming pelagic creatures and the denizens of various bottom communities including the reefs themselves. Most reef creatures in fact have planktonic eggs and/or larvae. This method of dispersal underlies both the widespread geographic distribution of most reef organisms and the ability of reefs to rapidly recover their populations when devastated by storms or other disasters.

At the bottom line all sustainable systems must balance their books. The harvest of plankton by reefs is balanced by their contribution of eggs, larvae, and organic debris to the water as it leaves them. Energy, ultimately derived from the nuclear incandescence of the sun, is the real harvest. The nutrient molecules essential to storing such energy are simply exchanged.

Life drifting weightless in a fluid environment without a substrate has afforded plankton the ultimate freedom of design.

Some plankters have assumed the shape of spheres, cubes, rectangles, triangles and other geometric forms. Transparency is common. Certain jellyfishes are only slightly less fluid than the water itself. They literally pour into formlessness if lifted from their supporting medium. Feathery appendages and unwieldy spikes and spines are frequent accoutrements. Colonial creatures link up in gossamer chains.

The planktonic stages of most bottom dwellers are not simply small versions of the adults, but like caterpillar and butterfly, radically and unrecognisably different. Only when they find a suitable substrate and settle down do they transform into a recognisable juvenile version of their parents.

Reef creatures feeding on such a diverse food source employ a variety of techniques. Filtering is used by sponges, bivalves, and sea squirts to capture the smallest plankton. Grasping tentacles and tendrils are used by corals, anemones, certain sea cucumbers, and basket starfish for slightly larger plankton.

Reef fishes depend upon keen eyesight to pick out individual plankters of their choice. Among the exotic specialists are the flashlight fishes. They are cloaked in black and equipped with their own brightly luminescent headlights for night plankton feeding.

Among the reef planktivores is one surprising group who would themselves normally be considered as plankton. These are mainly certain small polychaete worms and species of minute crustaceans. The worms emerge from the substrate at night and swim rapidly about over the reef. The crustaceans, mainly copepods and mycid shrimps, form shoals which shelter on the reef and manage to avoid being swept away by currents. Somehow they also manage to avoid being instantly devoured by plankton-feeding fishes who seem to ignore them.

A CONSTELLATION OF PLANKTON – RADIOLARIA AND DINOFLAGELLATES.

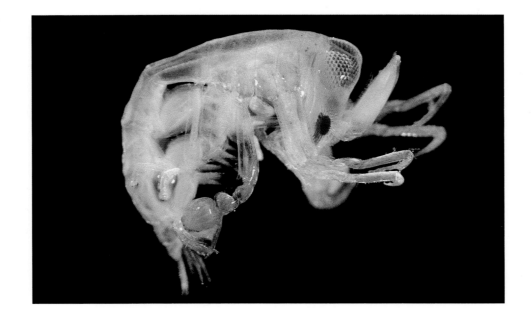

PHRONIMA, A PLANKTONIC PREDATOR THAT LIVES INSIDE ITS PREY.

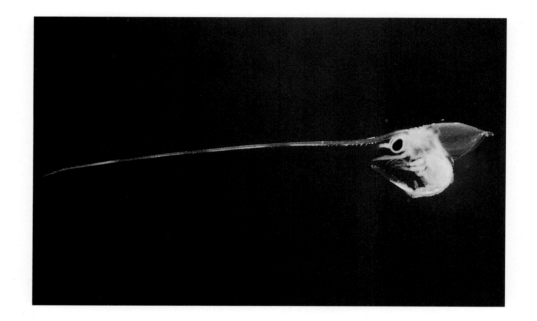

LANCELOT LARVAE, AN EARLY STAGE OF A PORCELLANID CRAB.

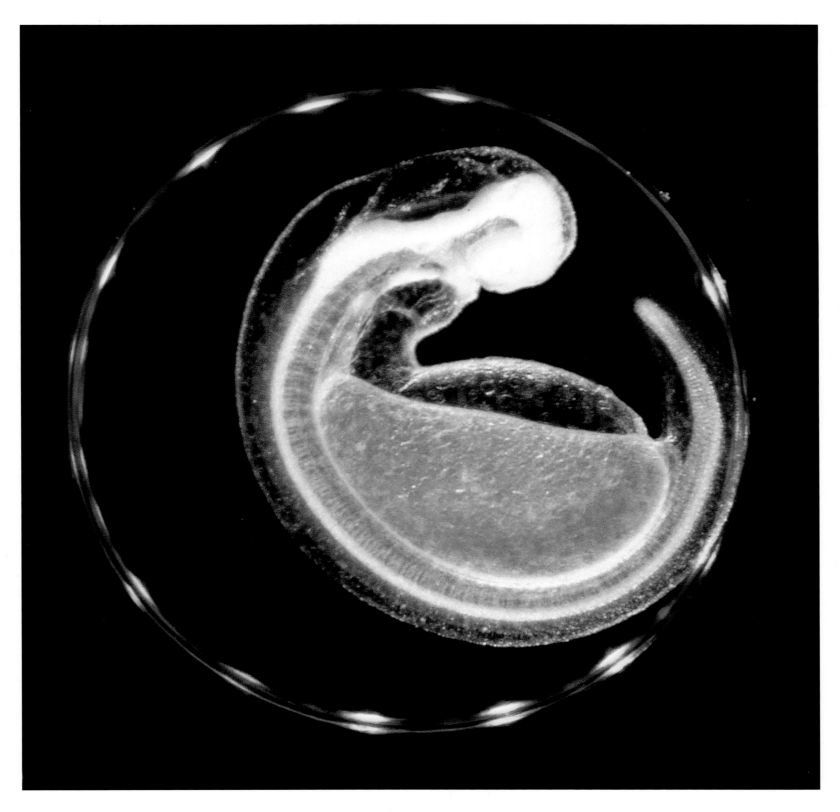

EEL EGG WITH DEVELOPING EMBRYO.

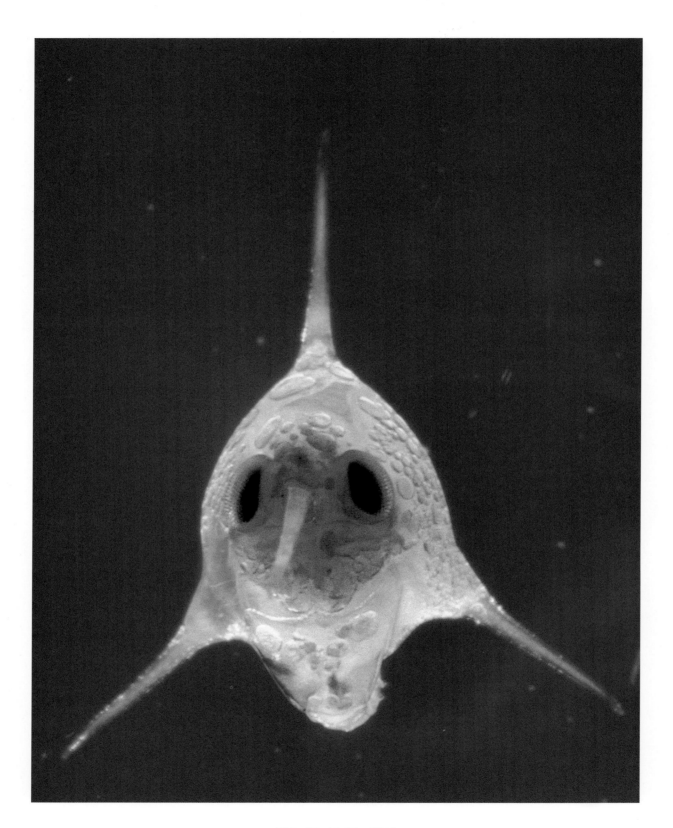

ZOEA STAGE OF A CRAB.

A LARVAL HERMIT CRAB.

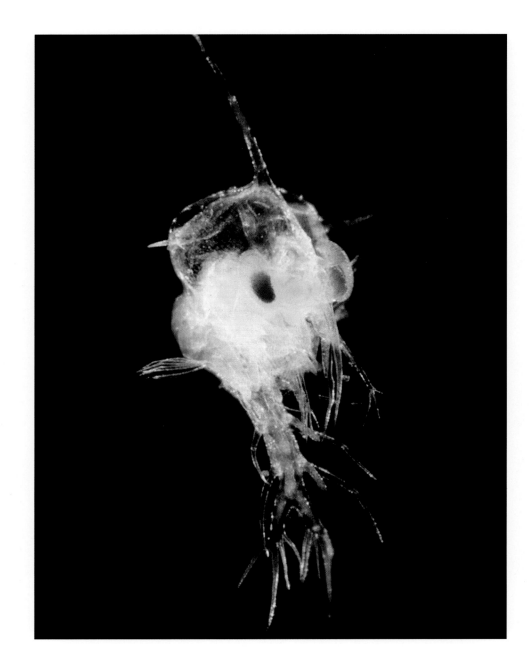

ANOTHER CRAB ZOEA.

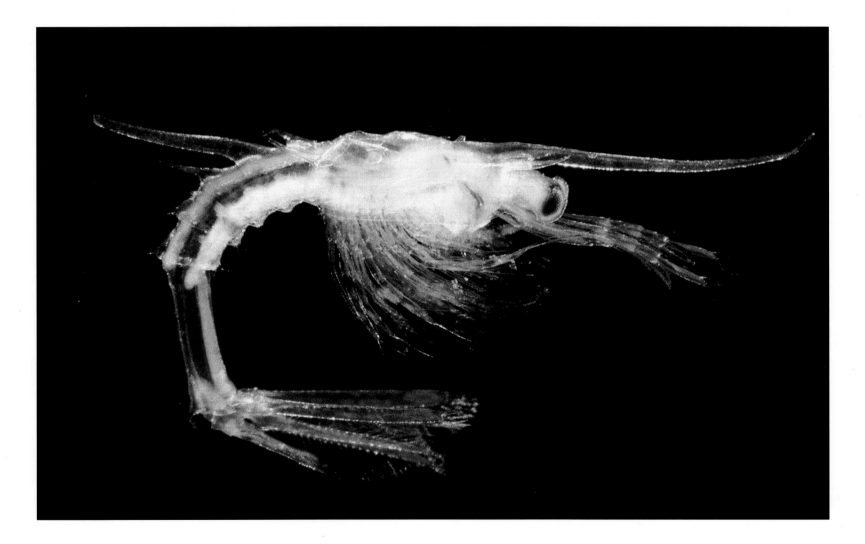

TROPICAL SHRIMP LARVAE.

PLANKTONIC AMPHIPOD CRUSTACEAN.

THE OPAL COPEPOD.

LIVING FIREWORKS, THE SURFACE DRIFTING *PORPITA*.

GLAUCUS, A PLANKTONIC NUDIBRANCH.

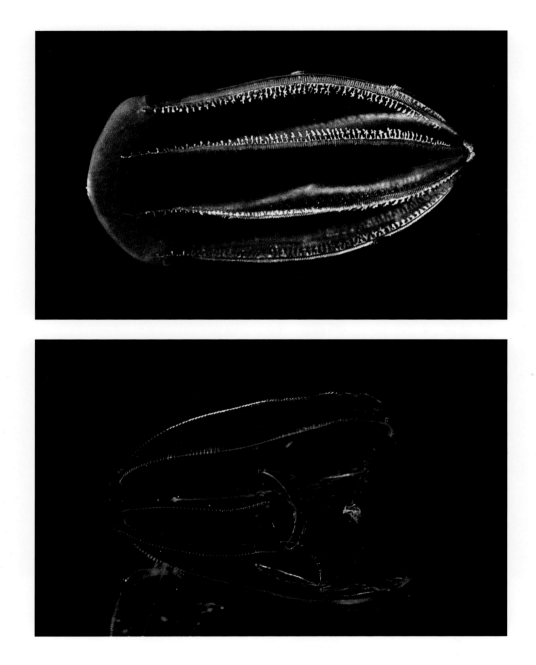

LIFE IN CRYSTAL, A COMB JELLY.   FLICKERING FIRELIGHT, ANOTHER COMB JELLY.

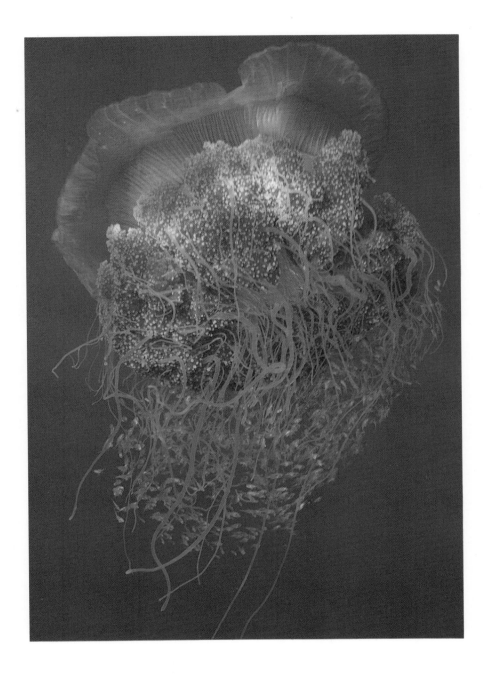

A PLANKTONIC GIANT. JELLYFISH WITH ATTENDANT FISHES.

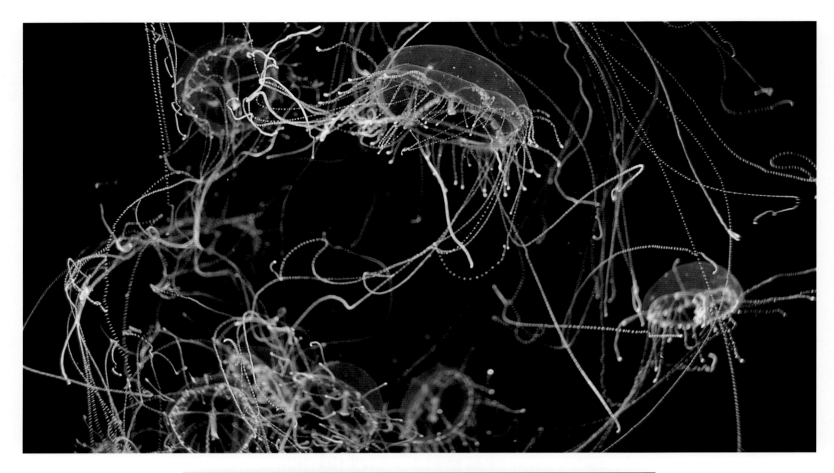

CIGAR JELLY BY NIGHT.   CIGAR JELLY BY DAY.

WALL OF MOUTHS. PLANKTON-FEEDING FISHES.

A BRANCHING CORAL RADIATES AN AURA OF PLANKTON FEEDERS.

FLOWER OF DOOM. A PLANKTON DEVOURING ANEMONE BLOSSOMS AT NIGHT.

Sand Community

The colour, conspicuousness, and abundance of life on reefs so dominates our experience of them it is easy to overlook its more subtle manifestations. The fauna of the sandy areas is an example. Like deserts on land, the sand areas of reefs appear at first glance to be rather barren and lifeless. Like their terrestrial counterpart, however, they harbour a surprisingly rich but largely hidden fauna with its own special beauty and fascination.

The sand itself is a product of the reef community. It is composed of fragments of the hard parts of numerous reef organisms. Shells and coral ground up by wave action and the feeding activities of reef animals are especially prominent as is the calcified leaves of the green algae *Halimeda*. Teeth and otoliths (ear bones) of fishes, spicules of sponges and soft corals, shells of crustaceans, tests and spines of sea urchins, and bits of sundry other creatures add their contribution. Sand is a major component of coral reefs. A large portion of the bottom on and around most reefs is covered with sand.

Sand, fallen from the outer slopes of reefs, frosts the ledges of the dropoffs and accumulates in a talus slope far below. It lines the bottom of surge channels, makes a patchwork with the coral of the reef flat, and creates rippled plains in the back reef area. Behind the reef it spills down dune-like slopes into the lagoon where it blankets the floor in a smooth carpet. Here and there waves and currents conspire to heap it up into islets adding still another dimension to life on reefs.

Unlike deserts, these sand areas never lack water and food is not so sparse. Plankton and organic detritus from the reef bring a continuous flow of nutrition. There is also often a surprisingly productive film of microscopic algae on the surface of the sand. Only shelter from predation is lacking.

Reef creatures have employed a variety of adaptations to exploit this abundant habitat. Camouflage, heavy armoured shells, burying and burrowing are common methods of coping with the lack of shelter. Many sand dwellers are also nocturnal to add another impediment to predation.

Though inconspicuousness is the rule for life amid plain surroundings where shelter is minimal, the sand dwellers often exhibit their own special but subtle variety of beauty. Not for them the bold and gaudy vestments of the coral inhabitants, but instead they utilise pastels and tiny intricate details only visible close up.

Form, too, has been shaped by the sand. Eels with strong, wiry bodies and pencil-point noses, razorfishes with compressed bodies and sharp-edged foreheads, crabs with spade-like claws, and sea urchins with short bristle-like spines are all adaptations for burying in loose sand.

While the seething gaudy life of the coral areas overwhelm the eye and brain with a flood of input fairly screaming for attention, a few metres away the sand areas provide a welcome oasis of simplicity and solitude where only by choice of attention does a subtle realm reveal itself.

BANDED SNAKE EEL EMERGING FROM THE SAND.

COLONY OF GARDEN EELS.   INDIVIDUAL GARDEN EEL FROM THE SAME COLONY.

DESERT BLOOM. A TUBE ANEMONE ON THE LAGOON FLOOR.

TUN SHELL. A GIANT SNAIL OF THE REEF SANDS.

MALE ELEGANT SAND DIVERS IN COMPETITIVE DISPLAY.

SPINECHEEK GOBY, A RAINBOW HUED RESIDENT OF THE SAND.

THE SPECKLED GRUBFISH, A ROVING PREDATOR.

ELEGANT FIRE GOBY.

NOCTURNAL FORAGERS OF THE SAND COMMUNITY RESTING BY DAY.

A SILVER PHALANX OF BARRACUDAS ON PATROL.

BARBELS OF THE GOATFISH ARE USED TO PROBE THE SAND FOR FOOD.

THE SUCCESSFUL RESULT OF A FLOUNDER'S CAMOUFLAGE.

TURTLE NURSERY ON AN ISLAND OF REEF SAND.

LIFE AND DEATH. A NESTING TURTLE FAILS TO RETURN TO THE SEA.

Mimicry and Camouflage

Deception is a highly developed art on coral reefs. It ranges from the familiar type of mottled camouflage patterns to elaborate and precise mimicry of the colours, form, and motion of other creatures. The effectiveness of such deception may be extraordinary. Some is virtually impossible to detect even at close range in good light.

Perhaps the simplest form of camouflage is found among fishes which roam freely in the water column above the reef. They face the problem of appearing against varying backgrounds. The elegantly simple solution is their silvery sides which mirror their surroundings.

At the opposite extreme is the detailed camouflage of fishes such as scorpionfishes, flounders, flatheads, and wobbegong sharks. Some species have added elaborate leafy appendages as well to further aid in blending with marine growth.

Probably the ultimate masters of camouflage are the cuttlefishes (Sepia spp.). Their bodies are covered with a dense microscopic stippling of pigmented cells called chromatophores. Different cells contain different colours and each cell can expand or contract to reveal or hide its pigment. These cells are controlled by a nervous system under the direction of a well-developed brain perceiving its surroundings through a sophisticated eye. In the blink of one's eye a cuttlefish can totally alter its colour pattern to produce an uncanny match with its surroundings.

This instantaneous ability to faultlessly mix and match, however, is only one side of their mastery of disguise. They also have an amazing ability to mime shapes. For example, they can arrange their arms like coral branches, raise five-centimetre knobby appendages like more branches on their body, and assume the colour and polyp pattern of a coral. All this takes only a second or two. To the human eye the result is virtually indistinguishable from a real coral.

Cuttlefishes bridge the distinction between camouflage and mimicry. With camouflage, animals attempt to blend inconspicuously with their background whether it is a general one or a portion of another organism. Mimics boldly assume the guise of another creature in its entirety. The sinister case of the mimic cleaner wrasse has been mentioned in the introduction.

Most reef mimics are fishes. Blennies are particularly prone to this form of deception and one particular group of blennies has also afforded a popular range of models for other blennies to emulate. The models are the sabretooth blennies of the genus *Meiacanthus*. They are unique in possessing venomous fangs. This defensive capability presumably affords them a degree of immunity from predation, hence their popularity with mimics.

For other blennies, this particular mimicry is relatively easy. They already possess the right body shape and style of swimming from their common blenny heritage so all they have to do is assume the colour pattern of their model. Being mistaken for a sabretooth blenny, however, is such a good lurk that other unrelated fishes have gotten into the act as well. Some species of sabretooths have ended up as models for as many as three or four different mimics from as many different families of fishes. There are numerous variations on the theme. One surgeonfish (*Acanthurus pyroferus*) is a mimic only as a juvenile when it mimes certain species of angelfishes. The angelfishes are each totally different in colour and have differing geographic distributions. Unlike cuttlefishes, the surgeonfish cannot change its pattern at will but develops it when it settles down on a reef after its planktonic infancy. Somehow it must develop the right pattern to match the angelfish species in its area.

How this is achieved is unknown, beyond the present frontier of knowledge which confronts us everywhere on coral reefs.

THE CLEANER WRASSE REMOVES PARASITES FROM OTHER FISHES AND ENJOYS FREEDOM FROM PREDATION.

THE SABRETOOTH BLENNY MIMICS THE CLEANER FISH.

WHICH END IS THE HEAD? THE WEED WHITING CONFUSES ITS PREDATORS.

THE SADDLED PUFFERFISH IS POISONOUS FOR OTHERS TO EAT.

THIS FILEFISH IS A NON-POISONOUS MIMIC OF THE SADDLED PUFFERFISH.

ANOTHER MIMIC OF THE SADDLED PUFFER IS THE JUVENILE FOOTBALLER TROUT.

THE SIGNAL GOBY DISPLAYS A FALSE PAIR OF EYES.

DECOY SCORPIONFISH WITH MIMIC FISH DESIGN IN DORSAL FIN.

FILEFISH CAMOUFLAGED TO MATCH A GORGONIAN.

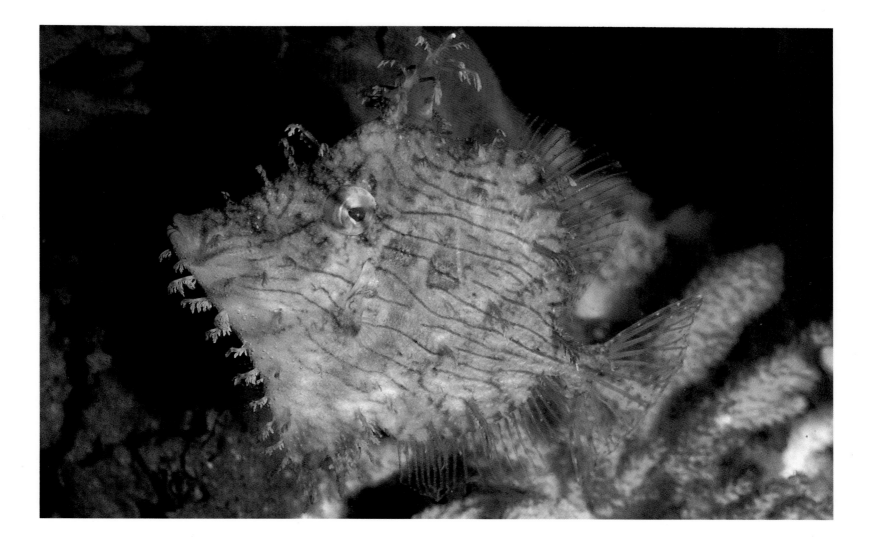

TASSELS ENHANCE THE CAMOUFLAGE OF THE PRICKLY LEATHER-JACKET.

SPIDER CRAB WITH GORGONIAN CAMOUFLAGE.

A DECEPTIVELY CAMOUFLAGED DECORATOR CRAB.

THE OCTOPUS, A MASTER OF DISGUISE.

SARGASSUMFISH AWAY FROM ITS HOME OF FLOATING WEED.

A GHOST PIPEFISH AMID SOFT CORAL.   GHOST PIPEFISH AWAY FROM SHELTER.

THE LEAFY SEA DRAGON, PERHAPS THE MOST SPECTACULAR OF FISHES.

Living Together

A unique profusion of highly evolved commensal relationships is one of the more remarkable aspects of the manifold wonders of life on coral reefs. Survival of the fittest amid an atmosphere of unfettered competition was a somewhat naive and simplistic nineteenth century idea of natural selection which remains a popular conception of life in nature. Reality is somewhat different. Competition frequently occurs but is by choice more often avoided than engaged in. Toleration is the norm and active co-operation is not uncommon. In many instances this has led to specialised relationships in which quite different creatures live together with one or both benefiting and with no harm to either. Biologists call this commensalism, from the Latin for sharing the same table.

The abundance and diversity of life on coral reefs co-existing in close proximity for aeons has led to a multitude of commensal relationships. With vast spans of time in which to refine and shape it, commensalism on reefs often involves striking adaptations of colour and form as well as behaviour. Nowhere else in nature are commensals so abundant and so specialised.

Sponges, anemones, corals, sea urchins, feather starfishes, starfishes, clams, and, in fact, virtually all of the prominent attached and slow-moving fauna of the reef, have various special-ised commensals living with them. Numerous small caridean shrimps have, in particular, opted for a commensal way of life but there are a multitude of other types as well. There are commensal crabs, snapping shrimps, bryozoans, sponges, anemones, flat-worms, snails, fishes, and even a combjellyfish. Most are small creatures living harmlessly in the shelter of a larger host but there are many, too, who participate in arrangements which involve more obvious mutual co-operation and benefit. The latter include the well known clownfish and anemone relationship, the small fishes and shrimps who remove parasites from larger fishes, and the numerous paired species of gobies and snapping shrimps. The small commensals living on larger hosts frequently exhibit striking colour patterns quite unlike those of their independent non-commensal relatives. In isolation these patterns may seem quite bizarre, but in their natural setting they can be seen to be derived from small details of the appearance of the host where-upon they serve as effective camouflage. Form, too, has been moulded by the influence of commensalism. A tiny shrimp has evolved an elongate spindle shape and short hooked legs for living on the needle-like spines of the black sea urchin. The first dorsal fin of remoras has been reformed into a suction cup for clinging to host fishes. Pearlfishes have assumed a smooth, slender, elongate tear-drop shape to slip into and out of the body orifices of their host sea cucumbers and oysters.

For most reef commensals, their relationship has evolved to the point that it is obligatory. Though the larger host may occur without its commensals, the commensals are never found apart from the host. In some, neither partner is ever without the other.

ALLIED COWRIE AND SOFT CORAL HOST.

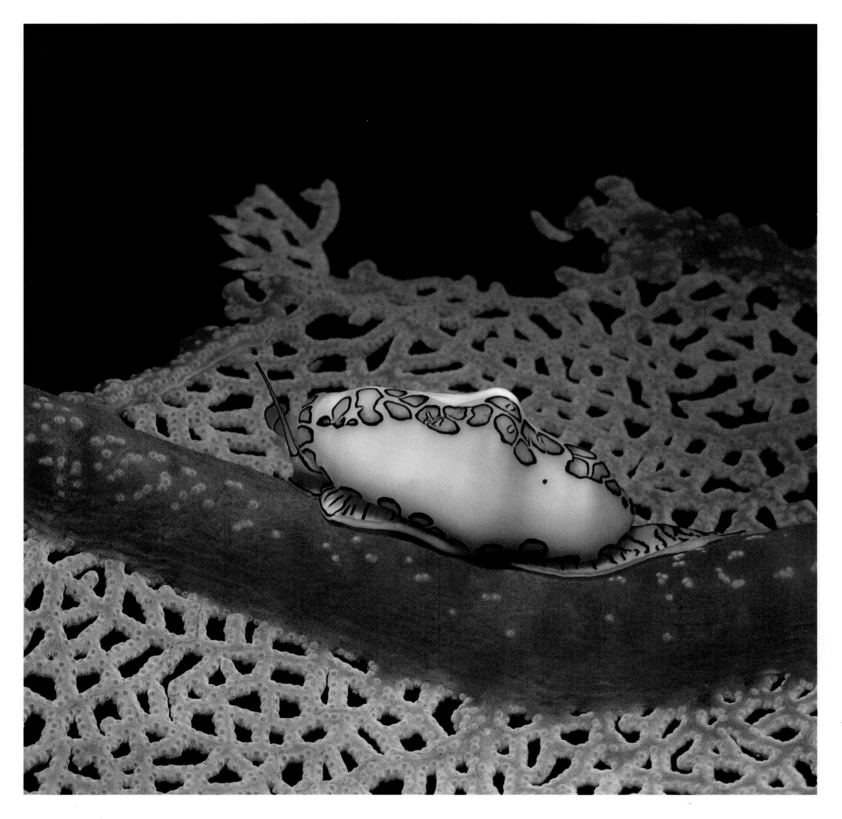

FLAMINGO TONGUE LIVING ON A SEA FAN.

IMPERIAL SHRIMPS ON SPANISH DANCER NUDIBRANCH.

SPANISH DANCER NUDIBRANCH SWIMMING.

NEEDLE SHRIMP ON URCHIN SPINE.

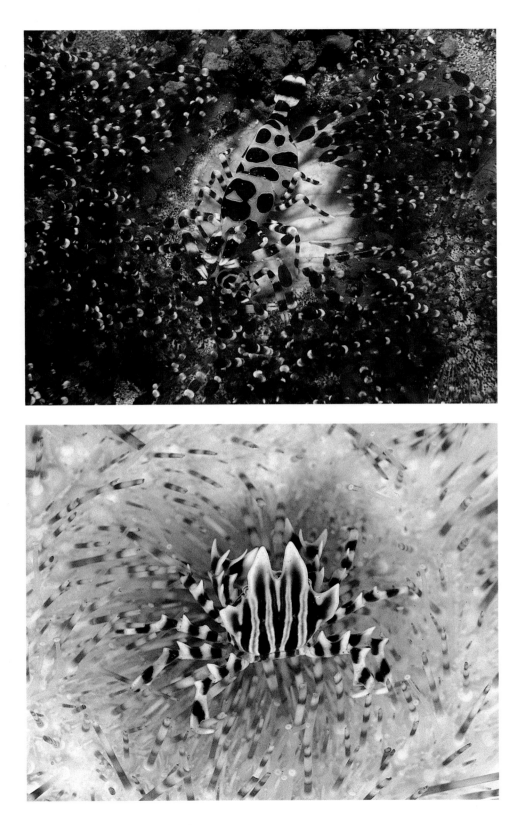

COLEMAN'S SHRIMP PAIR ON VENOMOUS URCHIN.   ZEBRA CRAB ON SEA URCHIN.

ELEGANT SQUAT LOBSTER ON FEATHER STARFISH HOST.

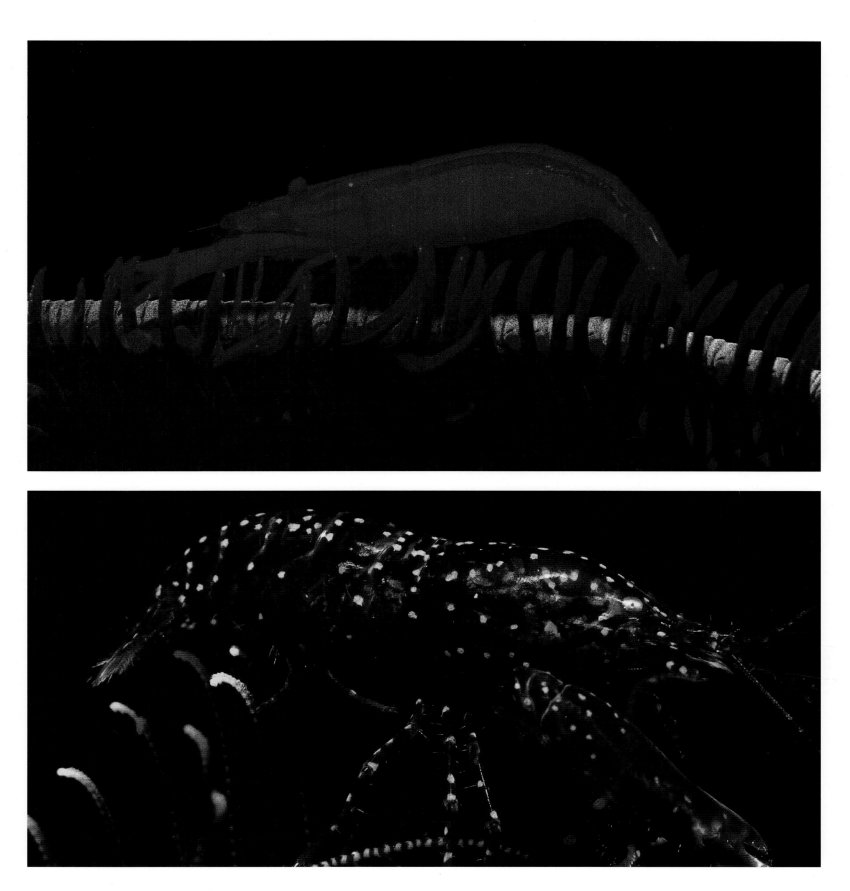

COMMENSAL SNAPPING SHRIMP ON FEATHERSTAR.   PONTONIINE SHRIMP WITH FEATHERSTAR HOST.

LYSMATA CLEANING SHRIMP SERVICING CORAL COD.

LYSMATA CLEANING SHRIMP SERVICING MORAY EEL.

A COMMENSAL CLASSIC, THE ANEMONE FISHES.

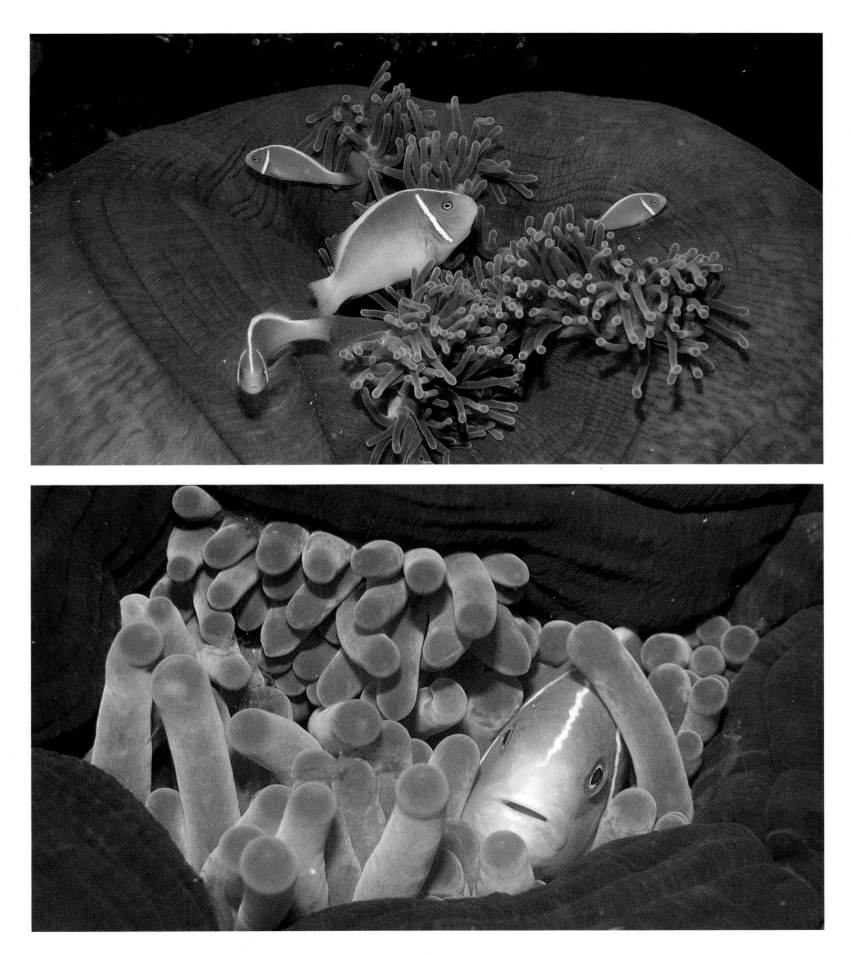

THE CLOWN ANEMONEFISH

SPINECHEEK ANEMONEFISH.

ANEMONE CRABS WITH HOST. EGGSHELL SHRIMP ON ANEMONE. APPALOOSA SHRIMP ON CORAL.

HARLEQUIN CRAB WITH ITS PROTECTIVE HOST. FISTS OF FURY. A BOXER CRAB WITH ANEMONE GLOVES.

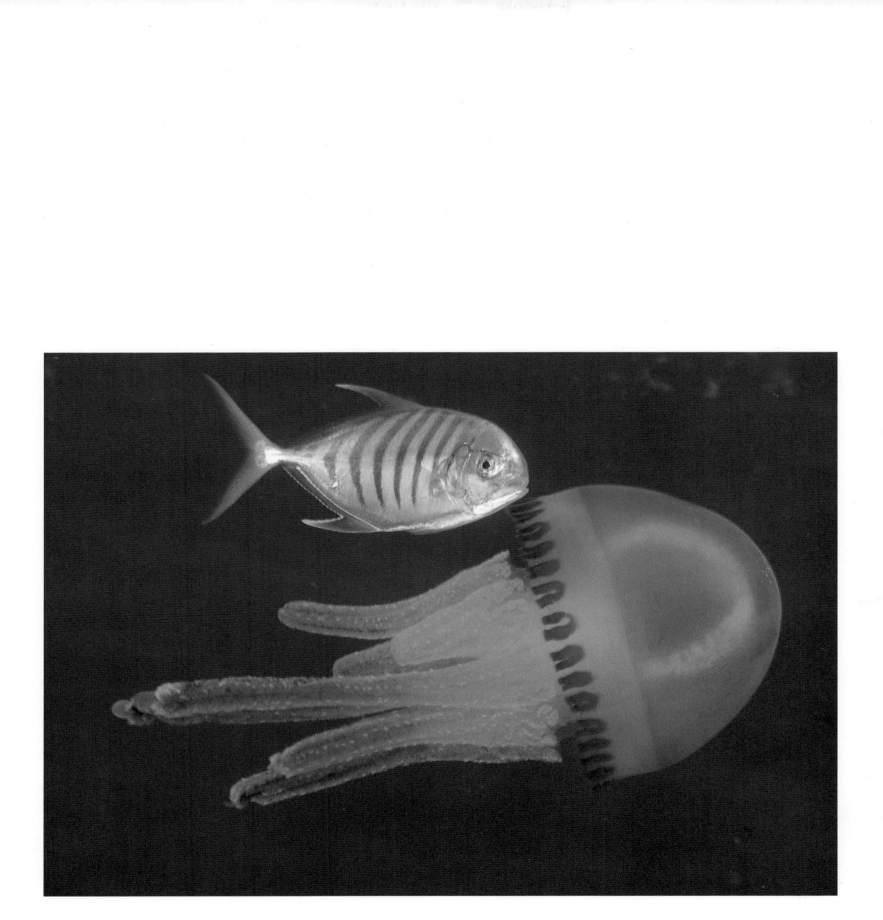

YOUNG BLUE TREVALLY SHELTERING WITH JELLYFISH.

GOBY AND SNAPPING SHRIMP COMMENSAL RELATIONSHIPS.

Armaments and Defence

Coral reefs are a realm of predators. Cold blooded and living in a weightless environment, their requirements for energy are low so there can be many more of them in relation to their prey than is found in terrestrial communities. This abundance of predators has led to an evolutionary arms race resulting in a proliferation of exotic means of defence.

The defence armamentarium of reef creatures includes a broad spectrum of methods including chemical, physical, and behavioural. Simple organisms such as algae, sponges, corals, flatworms, and nudibranchs have frequently opted for chemical defence involving substances which make them distasteful or poisonous to eat. More complex creatures have enhanced the effectiveness of defensive toxins by evolving means of applying them without themselves having to be bitten or eaten. Boxfishes and some sea cucumbers, for example, can exude poison into the water around them if disturbed. More commonly spines or fangs are employed to inject a painful venom. This method is particularly popular with fishes, especially the scorpionfishes and their relatives, but sea urchins, the crown-of-thorns starfish, cone shells, and other creatures also have venomous capabilities.

Armour and spines are perhaps the most widespread of the physical means of defence. The shells or molluscs and spines of fishes are ubiquitous examples. Mollusc shells have not only made their owners a dominant group, but they have also spawned another successful group, the hermit crabs, who use them after their original owners have died. Spines occur in a wide variety of specialised forms. The stony skeletons of corals are embellished with multitudes of tiny sharp blades and spikes to lacerate the mouths of any would-be coral eaters. Bristleworms are equipped with tufts of microscopic glass-like spines which are highly irritating if touched. Sea urchins bristle with long, brittle, toxic spines of needle sharpness. Lionfishes too, have needle-like spines. Theirs have a groove which conducts venom from a gland at the base of each spine. Porcupine pufferfishes are covered with stout spines which they can erect by inflating their body with water thus turning themselves into a drum-tight sphere of spikes.

Other physical methods of defence include speed, electricity, sound and colour. Streamlining and speed enable small plankton-feeding fishes to move up into the open water above the reef to feed, but flee rapidly back to shelter if a predator approaches. Electric rays can generate a shock of about 100 volts to deter predators. Snapping shrimps use specialised claws to produce an explosive sound which can stun small fishes. Colour is utilised both in the form of camouflage to achieve invisibility and as strikingly conspicuous warning patterns associated with toxic properties. The toxin may be either the bearers own or even that of another species which is being mimicked.

Behaving in a manner which minimises the danger from predation is a highly developed art among reef dwellers. Successful camouflage and mimicry, as well as living as a commensal in the shelter of another creature, all involve specialised behaviour. Constructing a burrow for safe retreat, hiding, sticking close to shelter, and emerging only under cover of darkness are also common methods of avoiding predation. Small plankton-feeding fishes adjust the distance they will venture away from the coral according to light, water clarity, current, and the presence of predators. Like pulsing auras, their shoals expand out from the coral and contract back to it with each passing predator.

Shoals in themselves are also an effective means of defence. To make a successful attack, a predator must fix its attention on one individual and compensate for its evasive tactics. Shoals huddle closely together and mill about when threatened making it difficult to fix on any one fish.

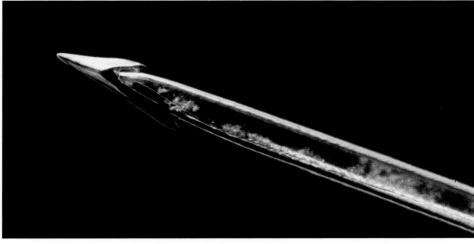

THE TEXTILE CONE IS EQUIPPED WITH A QUIVER OF POISON DARTS.

A FLAT BODY PERMITS THIS HERMIT CRAB TO LIVE IN A CONE SHELL.

AN INFLATED PORCUPINEFISH BECOMES AN INEDIBLE BALL OF SPINES.

VENOMOUS SPINES PROTECT THE CROWN-OF-THORNS STARFISH.

SPINY ARMOUR SURROUNDS THE MOUTH OF A SLATE PENCIL URCHIN.

A LIVING PINCUSHION. NEEDLE-LIKE SPINES PROTECT THE RADIANT STAR URCHIN.

THE SABRE SQUIRRELFISH IS ARMED WITH A VENOMOUS CHEEK SPINE.

DECORATIVE SYRINGES WARN OF THE LIONFISH'S POISON.

THE SPOTTED BOXFISH, A COLOURFUL LABELLED POISON CONTAINER.

A CLOWN TRIGGERFISH. ITS PATTERN IS DESIGNED TO WARN NOT AMUSE.

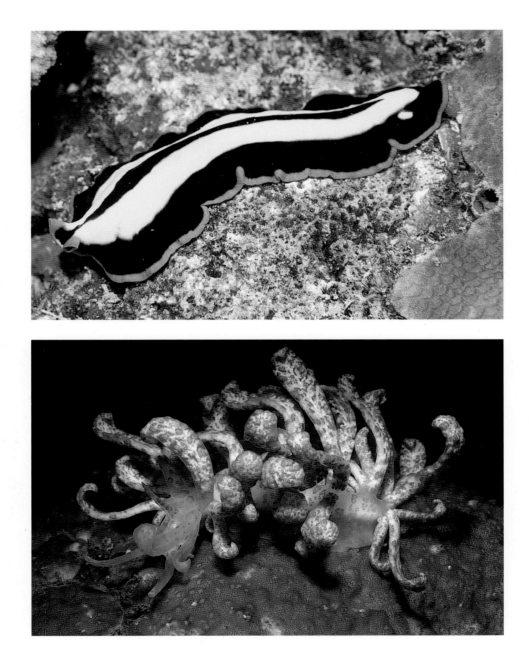

A FLATWORM, ANOTHER GAUDY EXAMPLE OF WARNING COLOURATION.   SACRIFICIAL DETACHABLE ARMS ARE THIS NUDIBRANCH'S DEFENCE.

DANGER ACCOMPANIES BEAUTY WITH THE WARNING COLOURS OF A NUDIBRANCH.

SAFETY IN NUMBERS. A SCHOOL OF BROWNSTRIPE SEAPERCH.

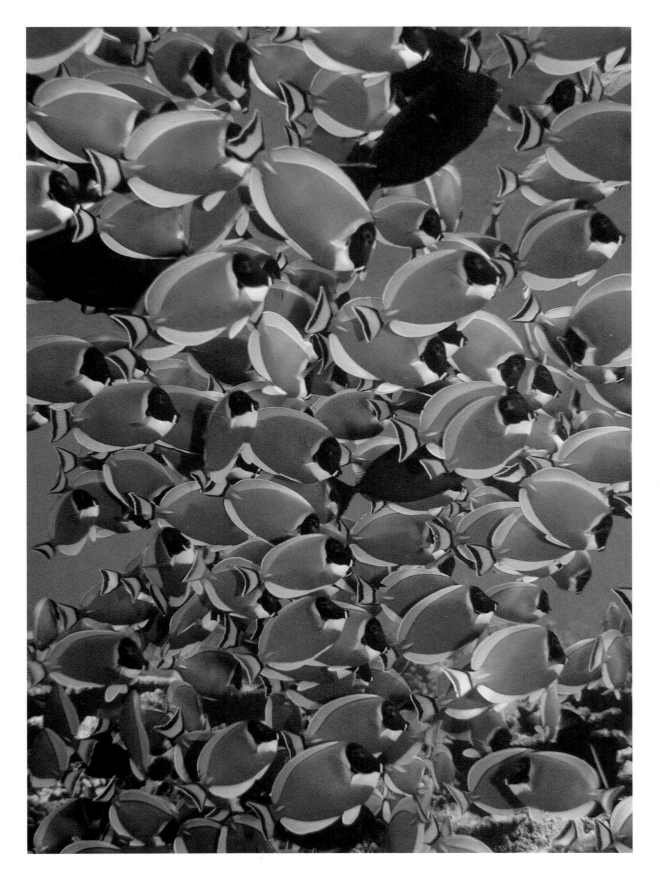

SURGEONFISHES UTILIZE SCHOOLING STRATEGY TO DECREASE THE CHANCE OF PREDATION.

WHEN ALL ELSE FAILS. THE FINAL DEFENCE OF A STARFISH IS TO REGENERATE ITSELF FROM A FRAGMENT.

STINGING TENTACLES OF A PORTUGUESE MAN-O-WAR.

TOP OF THE FOOD CHAIN. A TIGER SHARK HAS NOTHING ELSE TO FEAR.

Reproduction

As one might expect, reef creatures employ every conceivable means of reproduction. For the overwhelming majority, however, reproduction involves external fertilisation followed by a planktonic larval stage. Eggs and sperm are released to mix and fertilise, with most, or all, of early development taking place while drifting along with the currents. This method of reproduction carries the highly vulnerable early life stages away from the predator-filled reef environment and assures a wide dispersal of the offspring. Surviving the dangerous planktonic journey and ending up in a suitable reef habitat is, of course, a matter of chance against overwhelming odds. Success entails starting with large numbers of eggs, typically many thousands and often millions.

Various additional strategies are employed by different creatures to better the odds. For most, spawning takes place in the season of most favourable conditions in the plankton. It is also often synchronised with the lunar cycle to coincide with the strongest tidal currents and thus enhance dispersal of the eggs. On many Indo-Pacific reefs, corals and a variety of other creatures have an annual mass spawning. On the Great Barrier Reef this occurs at night just before moonrise, four or five nights after the full moon around November. At that time the entire reef erupts in a mass orgy of spawning. A blanket of floating eggs soon covers the surface and the clean sea air takes on a distinctive musky odour.

Another strategy for improving the odds involves parental protection of developing eggs until they hatch into planktonic larvae. The many species of damselfishes lay attached eggs which are guarded by the male who drives away potential egg eaters. In cardinalfishes the male carries the eggs in his mouth and forgoes eating until they hatch. Many gobies secrete their eggs in hidden nests. In most crustaceans they are carried beneath the abdomen of the female until they hatch.

Competition for food and shelter in the crowded reef community has led many reef fishes to become territorial. Larger, more aggressive males establish exclusive territories from which they drive away competitors and in which they accumulate harems of smaller females. In these species all individuals start life as females and later change into males only when they are large enough to defend their own territory. The females have their own pecking order and if something happens to the male, the dominant female may undergo a hormonal change and take his place. This system assures each individual the maximal opportunity to produce the greatest number of offspring. Apart from the majority with their planktonic larvae, there are a host of interesting specialisations. Many molluscs produce tough leathery egg cases which protect the developing embryo. Some hatch into planktonic larvae, others develop directly into tiny shelled juveniles. The latter case is especially prevalent among the innumerable micro-molluscs who live among the sand grains. They are too small to produce the large numbers of eggs necessary for success against the odds among the plankton and so must rely on direct development in their hidden niche in the sand. Limited distribution has led to explosive speciation. There may be several hundred species in a handful of sand and many of these differ from one reef area to another.

Internal fertilisation with the production of few but highly developed offspring, the familiar mode of land vertebrates, occurs on the reef mainly among the largest fishes, the sharks and rays. In some sharks there is a strange but not entirely inappropriate twist to this familiar pattern. In these species the first embryos to develop eat subsequent eggs and embryos as they are produced, thus beginning their predatory career with cannibalism of their younger siblings while still in the womb.

GIANT CLAMS MUST SYNCHRONIZE SPAWNING WITH OTHERS NEARBY.

SEA URCHIN ENVELOPED IN A SMOKY CLOUD OF SPAWN.

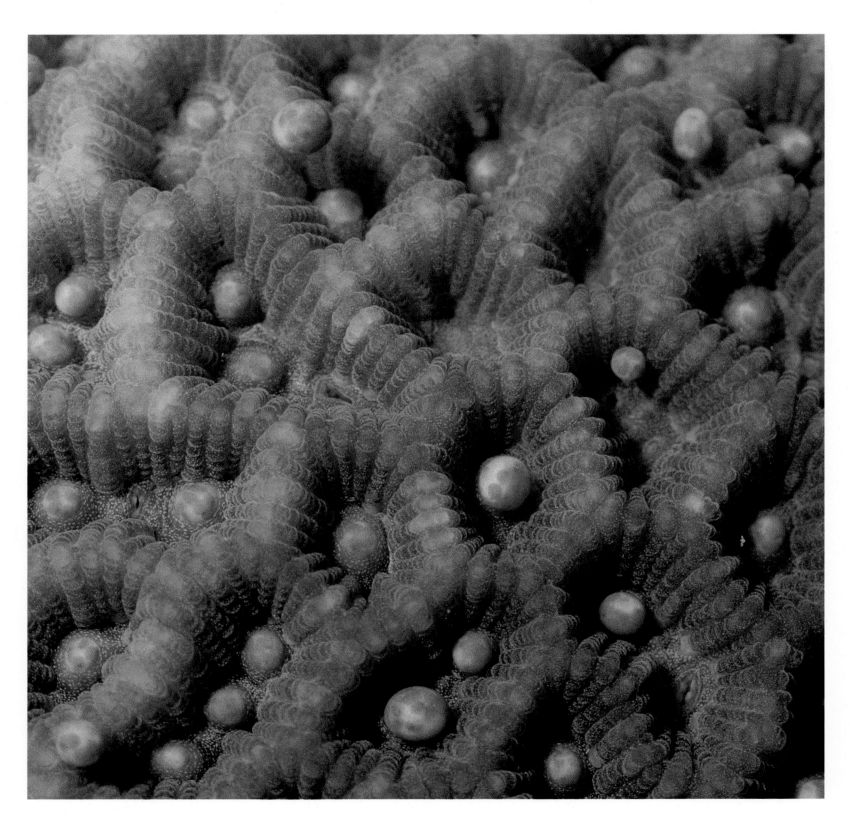

THE BIRTH OF A CORAL.

AN UPWARD RAIN OF CORAL EGGS.

EGGS BLANKET THE SEA AFTER A MASS CORAL SPAWNING.

CLEANER SHRIMP CARRYING ITS EGGS.

NUDIBRANCHS WITH THEIR EGG MASSES.

COLONIAL SEA SQUIRT COLONY.

LARVAE OF THE COLONIAL SEA SQUIRT.

CUTTLEFISH EGGS ATTACHED TO SPONGES.

ADULT CUTTLEFISH.

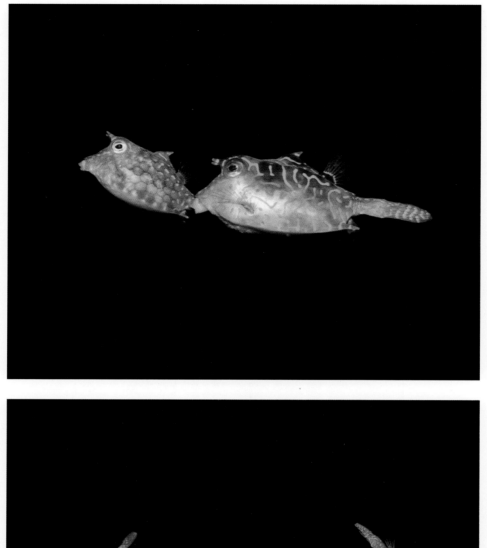

A FEMALE COWFISH LEADS A SPAWNING ASCENT.   AFTER SPAWNING, A RAPID DESCENT.

THE INSTANT OF SPAWNING. AN EXPLOSION OF EGGS AND SPERM.

SEAWHIP GOBIES SPAWNING. THEIR TRANSPARENT EGGS ARE ATTACHED TO THE WHIP UNDERNEATH AND BEHIND THE FISHES.

CARDINALFISH EGGS ARE CARRIED IN THE MOUTH OF THE MALE UNTIL HATCHING.

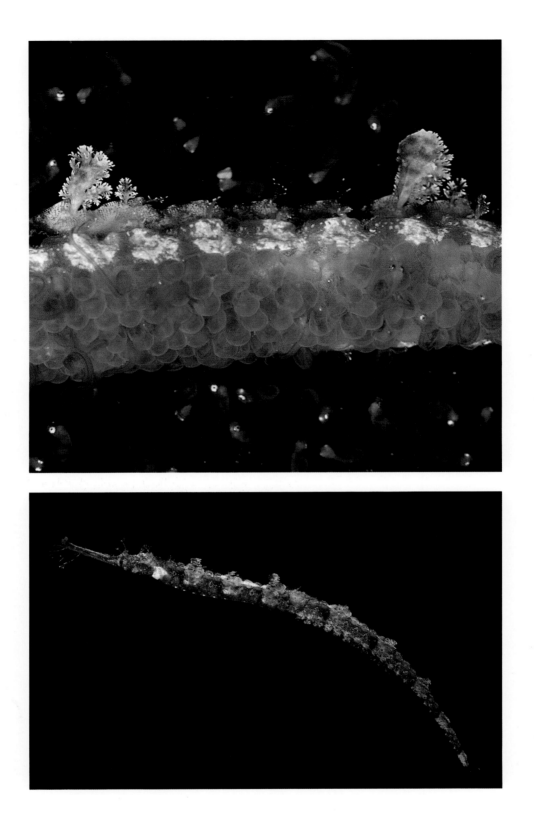

THE MOMENT OF BIRTH. PIPEFISH LARVAE HATCHING FROM EGGS CARRIED BY THE FATHER. THE EXPECTANT PIPEFISH FATHER JUST BEFORE THE EVENT.

MALE COURTSHIP FINERY. A DRAGONET DISPLAYS TO ITS MATE.

Colours and Adaptations

For sheer dazzling colour no other living thing equals the fishes of coral reefs. Their diversity, and boldness of patterns and range and brightness of colours, is unmatched by any other organisms. Adding to the visual delight, they are displayed on a wondrous array of forms accompanied by behaviour of endless variety.

Though our subjective perception of all this may be summated as beauty, the patterns and harmonies involved are largely related to practical needs. The functional reasons for most aspects of form and behaviour are usually not too difficult to discern. The amazing colours of reef fishes, however, have puzzled even many biologists. The function of these patterns can only be understood in their total context of origins, environment, way of life, and the visual physiology of their intended audience.

The audience is primarily other fishes. The visual capabilities of most invertebrates are either non-existent or too lacking in acuity to perceive much in the way of details. Reef fishes themselves, however, possess colour vision and have good acuity. Their colours serve three basic functions: concealment, confusion and advertisement.

Concealment or camouflage makes the individual hard to distinguish from its surroundings. This function is usually obvious but sometimes such patterns may appear striking when apart from their normal situation. This is especially true of commensals.

Confusion patterns lead the viewer to incorrectly perceive their wearer. False eye spots are commonly employed to misdirect attacks away from the real eye. Dark stripes hiding the eye often accompany such eye spots and are also used by predators to help conceal their attention. High contrast dazzle patterns break up their owner's outline and make both identification and orientation difficult to correctly interpret. Stripes, lines, and spots which make individuals difficult to distinguish in a shoal are also a commonly encountered confusion effect. Mimicry of another species is a special type of confusion colouration.

Most of the really striking colour patterns of reef fishes, however, are designed to be just that. They advertise the distinct identity of their owner. On a reef several hundred different fishes may be within sight of one another at once.

Despite the diversities of form and behaviour there are frequently as many as several dozen species of similar size, form and behaviour. Each species must deal with its own competitors and predators, find mates and avoid wasting its time and energy responding to the many species of no real concern to it. There is a need for instantaneous correct identification. There is also no way to browse, pick plankton, or guard a territory and remain truly inconspicuous. Coral affords an abundance of shelter for safe retreat if threatened. The result has been an unparalleled explosion of distinctive colour patterns whose primary function is to be clearly distinguished from all others.

Often the functions are not exclusive. The same pattern may be distinctive close up but at a short distance away the diffusion of light underwater may blend its elements into a camouflage. Conspicuous markings, especially on fins, may be able to be displayed or concealed as needed.

All this does not mean that the beauty involved may not also exist for its own sake. We share with fishes a brain designed to recognise patterns. It would hardly be surprising if they, like us, responded to, and preferred, those harmonious patterns we call beautiful. Perhaps by choice of mates, the beauty they possess they themselves created through their own preference for the beautiful.

MALE PARROTFISH SPORTING AN ALGAL MOUSTACHE.

THE SPLENDID HAWKFISH IS DISTINCTIVE CLOSE UP, CAMOUFLAGED AT A DISTANCE.

FACIAL MARKINGS WHICH OBSCURE THE EYE ARE COMMON IN REEF FISHES.

OCELLI OR FALSE EYE SPOTS ARE ANOTHER COMMON FEATURE OF REEF FISH PATTERNS.

THE BLUE RIBBON EEL WINS A PRIZE FOR EXOTICA.

THE APTLY NAMED DRAGON MORAY.

THE DAZZLING CONFUSION PATTERN OF A JUVENILE SWEETLIPS.

A JUVENILE RAZORFISH EMULATES SWAYING WEED.

MIX AND MATCH. A GOLDEN BLOUSE WITH A POLKA-DOT SKIRT.   THE SAILFIN TANG. ITS PATTERN EXAGGERATES HEIGHT AND HIDES THE EYE.

VIVID COLOURS OF THE FLAME ANGELFISH PROCLAIM OCCUPIED TERRITORY.

SUBTLE COLOURS FACILITATE RECOGNITION ONLY AT CLOSE RANGE.

A TARTAN PATTERN HELPS THIS HAWKFISH BLEND INTO GORGONIAN BRANCHES.

THIS FILEFISH CAN DISPLAY A STRIKINGLY MARKED VENTRAL SIGNAL FLAP.

NOCTURNAL REEF FISHES FREQUENTLY HAVE LARGE EYES AND RED COLOURATION.

ONLY THE MALE GILDED TRIGGERFISH HAS THE YELLOW MARGINS AND BLUE CHIN PATCH.

THE FLAG-LIKE PATTERN OF THIS SURGEONFISH PROCLAIMS TERRITORIAL SOVEREIGNTY.

BONY SCALES EMBEDDED IN A TOUGH LEATHERY SKIN UNDERLIE THE COLOURFUL PATTERN OF THIS TRIGGERFISH.

MALE LYRETAIL ANGELFISH. THE FEMALE LACKS THIS BARRED PATTERN.   IN A SCHOOL, THIS PATTERN BECOMES A SEETHING MASS OF LINES AND DOTS.

A JEWELLED TREASURE FROM THE CORAL KINGDOM, WHEELER'S SHRIMP GOBY.

THE REGAL ATTIRE OF THE ROYAL GRAMMA.

JUVENILE PARROTFISH WITH AN UNCHARACTERISTIC CONSPICUOUS COLOURATION.

THE LYRETAIL WRASSE, LIKE THE LYRETAIL ANGELFISH, HAS OPTED FOR A PLANKTIVOROUS LIFESTYLE.

THE SPLENDID DOTTYBACK MIXES A VARIETY OF ELEMENTS IN ITS COLOUR PATTERN.

HAWKFISHES PERCH MOTIONLESS AMID THE CORAL UNTIL PREY IS WITHIN STRIKING DISTANCE.

MALE LINESPOT WRASSE DISPLAYING COURTSHIP COLOURS.

DISTINCT FACIAL MARKINGS ARE EVIDENT ON MANY WRASSE SPECIES.

THE PSYCHEDELIC APPEARANCE OF A MANDARIN FISH.

THE BLUE TANG'S COLOUR MATCH MID-WATER WHERE IT FEEDS.

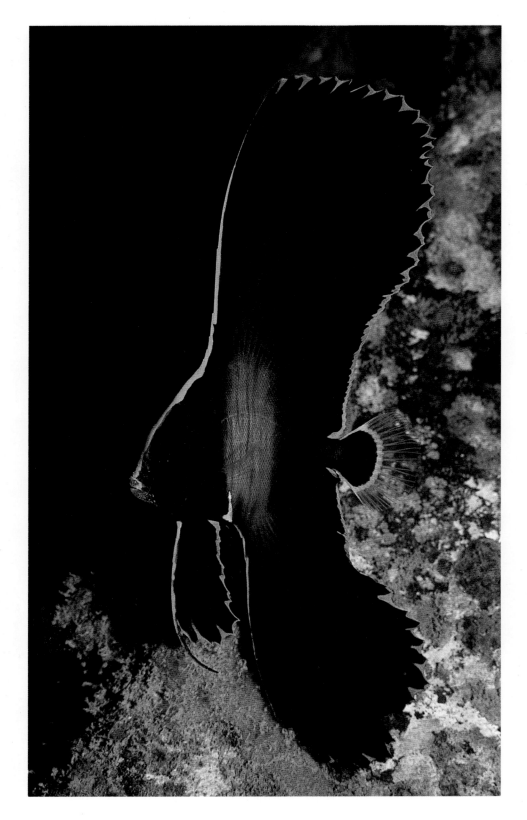

GOLD AND BLACK VELVET ADORN A JUVENILE BATFISH.

TUSKFISHES USE THEIR FORMIDABLE CANINE TEETH TO OVERTURN CORAL RUBBLE IN SEARCH OF FOOD.

Variations

Among reef fishes certain groups have evolved numerous species based on a particularly successful body plan. With multiple species of similar size and form, distinctiveness of colour pattern has become especially important. Angelfishes, butterflyfishes, damselfishes, fairy basslets, and parrotfishes are examples of such groups and their colours are among the most striking of any reef fishes.

Variations on a basic theme have yielded a seemingly endless variety of patterns. Each is distinctive yet also related by underlying denominators, a visual melody played in different keys on various instruments with each player's own interpretation. The dazzling variety of colouration in reef fishes is not restricted to differences between species. Even within a given species there may be distinctly different patterns corresponding to age, sex, habitat, activity, and even day or night. Small juveniles, due to their size, must often lead very different lives from adults and they frequently exhibit entirely different colouration. Males and females, especially in territorial and haremic species also lead quite different lives and many have brightly coloured males. In some species individuals from deeper water are distinctly reddish in overall colouration though this is not normally visible as red light is rapidly absorbed in water. Additional patterns may be turned on and off during courtship or feeding. Camouflage may be altered to match differing backgrounds. At night the bright colours of many fishes fade and they assume an irregular blotched or barred pattern. Both resting diurnal species and nocturnal species prowling alone in the open assume this type of camouflage. In a number of species there are occasionally golden or xanthic individuals of which neither cause nor function are known. In fishermen's legends they are attributed special powers.

Because the colour patterns of reef fishes are generally so distinctive, early ichthyologists often thought different coloured males and females or juveniles and adults were different species and bestowed upon them different scientific names. The parrotfishes in particular were subject to such confusion. It has only been in recent years with the widespread advent of scuba diving that biologists, observing what lives together and individuals in the process of transformation from one pattern to another, have finally linked up most of the patterns with their appropriate species.

One damselfish, the Spiny Chromis (*Acanthochromis polyacanthus*) exhibits a unique form of colour variation. Like other damselfishes, it makes a nest and guards its eggs until they hatch. Unlike all other damselfishes, however, the newly hatched fry do not go drifting off into the blue beyond. Instead, they gather in a tiny shoal which the parent fish continues to defend. This continues for a matter of weeks until the juveniles reach a size where they are able to cope on their own with life on the reef. The result is that each separate reef area has its own genetically isolated population with noticeable differences in colour patterns from one to another. Its basically black and white colouration ranges from all black to all white with numerous degrees and patterns in between.

DRAMATIC DIFFERENCES IN COLOUR DISTINGUISH THE NUMEROUS SPECIES OF BUTTERFLYFISHES.

SADDLED BUTTERFLYFISH. RACOON BUTTERFLYFISH.

COPPERBAND BUTTERFLYFISH.

REGAL ANGELFISH. ECLIPSING EVEN THE BUTTERFLYFISHES IN SPLENDOUR, ANGELFISHES ARE AMONG THE MOST COLOURFUL FORMS OF LIFE.

BLUE-GIRDLED ANGELFISH.

QUEEN ANGELFISH.

YELLOW-FACED ANGELFISH.

SCRIBBLED ANGELFISH.

CONSPICUOUS ANGELFISH.

BLUE DEVIL. THE BOLD PATTERNS OF TERRITORIAL REEF SPECIES ARE MORE SIMPLIFIED ON THE SMALLER DAMSELFISHES.

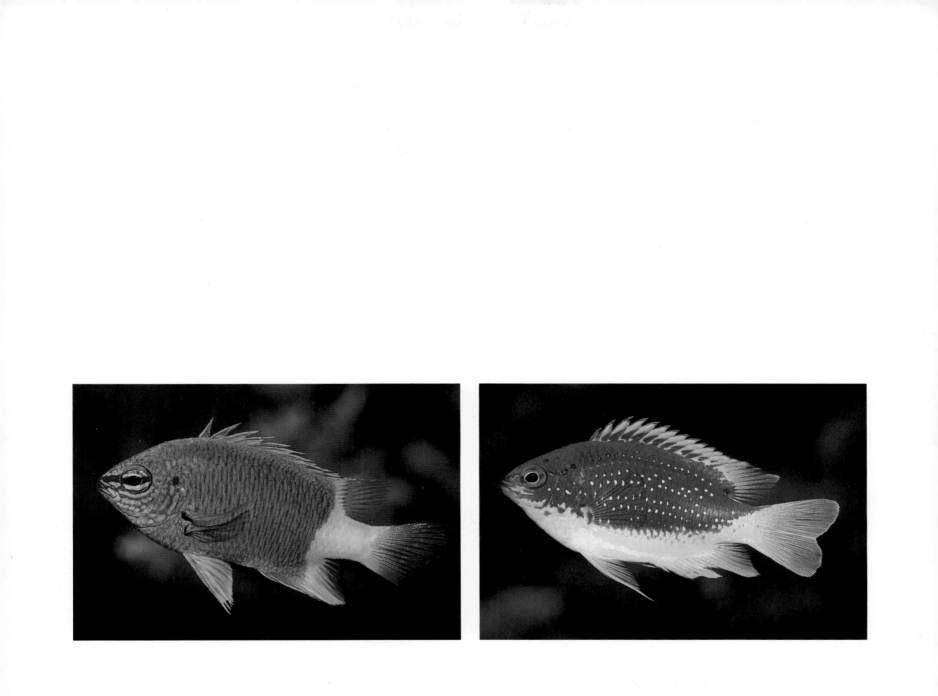

GOLDTAIL DEMOISELLE. SOUTHSEAS DEVIL.

JAVANESE DAMSEL. CROSS'S DAMSEL.

MULTISPINE DAMSEL

REDFIN BASSLET. SIMPLE PATTERNS ARE SUPPLEMENTED BY SMALL DISTINCTIVE MARKINGS AMONG THE BASSLETS.

STOCKY BASSLET. REDBAR BASSLET.

SCALEFIN BASSLET.

CAVE BASSLET. THREADFIN BASSLET.

PURPLE BASSLET.

PINK AND YELLOW BASSLET.

MALE AND FEMALE SQUARESPOT BASSLET. MALES AND FEMALES OF A NUMBER OF REEF FISHES HAVE DISTINCTIVELY DIFFERENT COLOURS.

AN UNUSUAL GATHERING OF MALE SQUARESPOT BASSLETS.

FEMALE TWINSPOT BASSLET.

MALE TWINSPOT BASSLET.

ADULT EMPEROR ANGELFISH. JUVENILES AND ADULTS OF SOME REEF FISHES ALSO HAVE DISTINCTIVELY DIFFERENT COLOURS.

JUVENILE EMPEROR ANGELFISH.

ADULT KING ANGELFISH.

JUVENILE KING ANGELFISH.

New Discoveries

The widespread advent of scuba diving in the 1950s began a unique new era of exploration and discovery. For the first time the underwater world became easily and directly accessible to mankind. Coral reefs, the richest, most beautiful and most fascinating of all natural communities, began to draw increasing attention from biologists. Permanent field stations and even full-fledged research institutions were established in coral reef areas.

The past three decades have seen an explosive growth in our knowledge of reef biology. To have participated in this era of the first human exploration of the richest of life's realms was a very special experience. The discovery of beautiful and exotic forms of life, the existence of which was previously unknown, was a regular occurrence. The witnessing of totally unsuspected behaviour and surprising interrelations came with almost every dive.

During this time it seemed that such revelations would go on forever but almost without noticing, the explosive rate of new discoveries has faded. Though our ignorance is still vast and much remains to be learned, the obvious has been noted. Future discoveries will increasingly be more subtle ones requiring more sophisticated effort.

Over this relatively short period several hundred previously unknown species of coral reef fishes were discovered. To one familiar with the known species in particular groups, it was often possible to recognise a new one at first sight. To be the first person to encounter a form of life that has successfully made its way unheralded through millions of generations, finally to appear to oneself alone, of all the inquisitive billions of our own kind, is one of life's more pleasantly exciting experiences. Ten years ago this thrill was commonplace. Now, far fewer fishes remain to be discovered.

In more obscure groups of organisms such as the micro-molluscs that live among the sand grains, scientifically unde-scribed species are still common. Their discovery, however, takes place through microscopes comparing specimens with those in museum research collections. Though this may be no less valid scientifically, as a personal experience it is not quite the same as finding and recognising the living creature in its own natural setting.

During the course of work for this book a number of previously unknown fishes and other organisms were photographed. Interestingly, creatures once discovered are often, in a short time thereafter, found in numerous other locations. It appears that once we are aware of something's existence and the type of situation in which to look for it, we begin to take notice of what previously slipped past our attention. It was often thus possible to locate and photograph for the first time, creatures only recently discovered at some other location thousands of kilometres away.

FOUR NEWLY DISCOVERED SAND-DWELLING GOBIES NOT YET SCIENTIFICALLY DESCRIBED AND NAMED.

ANOTHER RECENTLY DISCOVERED GOBY WITH A STRIKING DORSAL FIN.

EXQUISITE DENIZEN OF THE DEEP, THE LONGFIN BASSLET.

DISCOVERING THIS FISH WAS LIKE FINDING A LARGE AND PERFECT PRECIOUS STONE.

THIS TILEFISH EVADED DISCOVERY UNTIL RECENTLY BY DIVING INTO BURROWS.

THE PEACOCK-LIKE MALE COURTSHIP DISPLAY OF TWO RECENTLY DISCOVERED FILAMENT WRASSES.

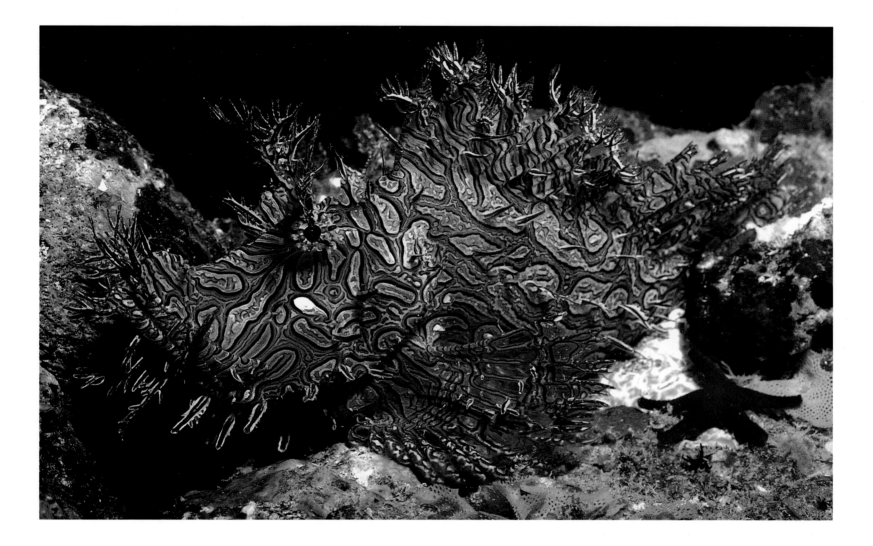

MERLET'S SCORPIONFISH. ITS UNIQUE CAMOUFLAGE HAS ENABLED ALL BUT A FEW SPECIMENS TO ESCAPE DETECTION.

RECENTLY DISCOVERED CRUSTACEANS. A CLEANER SHRIMP AND A REEF LOBSTER.

A SEA CUCUMBER NOT YET SCIENTIFICALLY NAMED.

RECENTLY PHOTOGRAPHED, AS YET UN-NAMED.

People and the Reef

Coral reefs have long played an important role in human affairs. For the island peoples of the Pacific, reefs were both a well stocked, easily accessible larder and a major cultural influence. Reef creatures supplied both the raw materials and the subject matter for extensive art, and via totemic animals, inspired much of the spiritual belief central to their entire existence.

To western man, reefs were first and foremost a deadly peril to mariners, a danger now only relegated to a lesser status but not eliminated by power and electronic methods of navigation. For a short period reefs supported the romantic pearl, *beche-de-mer*, and turtle fisheries as well as wrecking (that is, wreck salvaging).

Today, reefs are assuming an even wider and more important role for mankind. Reef-based tourism is growing rapidly and is already a multi-billion dollar worldwide industry affording enjoyment to millions. Their beauty has captivated multitudes of scuba divers fanatically addicted to the reef experience. Most are eventually tempted into the difficult and expensive hobby of underwater photography.

Scientifically, reefs afford unique opportunities to investigate and understand the phenomenon of life from manifold aspects. Reef creatures are also proving to be a cornucopia of biologically active compounds of potential pharmacological value. These range from substances which stimulate the immune system to anti-cancer drugs and an effective treatment for arthritis.

Perhaps the greatest importance of reefs to ourselves, however, is not economic or utilitarian but philosophical and spiritual They are a lesson by nature on life itself. On reefs we can immerse ourselves in its beauty and mystery. Like a magic elixir they seem to dissolve away the trivia which tend to ensnare us, and we can renew the awe and enthusiasm for life that we knew as children.

MAN-MADE ISLANDS IN THE SOLOMON ISLANDS.

THE LAST RESTING PLACE. REEF DWELLERS AND THEIR CLAMSHELL MONEY.

TOURISM HAS DISCOVERED THE WONDERS OF THE REEF.

A MAGIC CARPET RIDE ALONG THE EDGE OF A REEF ON A CALM DAY.

SCUBA DIVING AFFORDS AN INTIMATE EXPERIENCE OF CORAL REEFS.

EXPLORING INNERSPACE OFFERS FREEDOM OF MOTION IN THREE DIMENSIONS.

HAND FEEDING FISH AT THE COD HOLE ON AUSTRALIA'S GREAT BARRIER REEF.

SUNLIGHT AND GROTTOS CREATE NATURAL CATHEDRALS.

CORAL AND COCONUTS. A TROPICAL IDYLL.

A DISCARDED TRACKED VEHICLE.

AN ARMY JEEP. ITS TYRES ARE STILL INFLATED AFTER NEARLY HALF A CENTURY.

TRUCK USED BY U.S. FORCES.

A FLOAT BIPLANE USED FOR SCOUTING.

A JUNGLE TANK TUMBLES FROM THE HOLD OF A SUNKEN JAPANESE TRANSPORT.

U.S. HELLCAT FIGHTER DOWNED OFF NEW GEORGIA.

TWIN 50 CALIBRE TURRET GUNS OF A U.S. B17 FLYING FORTRESS.

Meet my Colleagues

Over the years I have had the pleasure of working with marine scientists from diverse fields. Let me introduce the personalities whose co-operation and assistance have stimulated my continued interest in life under the sea.

DR JOHN E. RANDALL, a living legend, is Curator of Fishes at the Bernice P. Bishop Museum in Honolulu and the foremost authority on the classification of tropical reef fishes. He was one of the first to use scuba apparatus as a research tool and still spends six months of the year on field trips. He has the world's largest collection of coral reef fish photos (some 4,000 species) and has discovered hundreds of fishes new to science.

DR WALTER A. STARCK II, a true pioneer of both scuba diving and underwater photography, received his doctorate from the University of Miami in 1964. He combined documentary film making with biological research and exploration in the Caribbean and Pacific oceans on his research vessel *El Torito* for more than 20 years. Since 1979 he has made a base in the tropical rainforest habitat on the Daintree River, north of Cairns, with easy access to the Great Barrier Reef.

DR GERALD R. ALLEN received a Ph.D. from the University of Hawaii in 1971. He is an authority on tropical Indo-Pacific reef fishes and has logged more than 3000 dives in over 40 countries in quest of fish specimens and underwater photos. He is the author of 15 books and over 160 scientific articles. Since 1974 he has held the position of Curator of Fishes at the Western Australian Museum in Perth.

PETER PARKS is a director and founding member of the much respected Oxford Scientific Films of England. He pursued a career of film-making specialising in nature and high magnification subjects for which he has won numerous awards. Although scientifically motivated, his talents have expanded into special effects and his work can be seen in films such as *Superman*, *Superman II*, *Alien*, and others. He has been involved with most major TV nature series in recent years and was principal contributor to *Life on Earth*.

Commentary

The scientific classification of many reef animals is still very incomplete. In some groups many species have not yet been described and given scientific names, and in others, the same species has been given different names at different times and places. As a result, it is not only impossible to provide accurate names for all of the organisms, but also some names used will undoubtedly be subject to revision in the future. In some cases, identification has been possible only at the level of family or order. Generic names are capitalised and in italics in accordance with scientific convention. Species names appear in lower case and italics. Where the genus is recognised but the species new or unknown, the generic name is followed by "sp.".

4 & 5. Aerial view of Vona Vona lagoon, Solomon Islands • photo, M. McCoy • Kodachrome

6 & 7. Lihou Reef, Coral Sea • Fujichrome

8 & 9. Russell Islands, Solomon Islands

10 & 11. Exposed corals on minus tides • Flynn Reef, Great Barrier Reef

12 & 13. Corals at Forbes Island, Great Barrier Reef • Fujichrome

34 Top. Bottlebrush acropora, *Acropora echinata* • Escape Reef, Great Barrier Reef • 10 metres

34 Left. Star coral, *Galaxea fascicularis* • Escape Reef, Great Barrier Reef • 8 metres

34 Right. Brain coral, *Leptoria phrygia* • Arlington Reef, Great Barrier Reef • 4 metres

35. Turret coral, *Tubastrea* sp. • Michaelmas Reef, Great Barrier Reef • 12 metres

There are approximately 800 species of reef building corals in the world. About 700 of these occur in the Indo-Pacific and 80 species are found in the Caribbean. Individual colonies of some of the larger corals have been recorded in excess of 40 metres wide.

36. Corals, *Acropora* and *Montipora* • Forbes Island, Great Barrier Reef • 3 metres • Fujichrome

The genus *Acropora* is a dominant group of reef corals comprising approximately 100 species. These are among the fastest growing corals and often make dense thickets of the branching forms. The plate-like forms may be up to three metres in diameter, and can reach a size over a metre in seven years. These fast growing corals tend to dominate regrowth of reefs devastated by storms or crown-of-thorns starfish.

37. Coral head and basslets: Cabbage coral, *Turbinaria reniformis*; coral at side, *Porites rus*; Scalefin basslet, *Pseudanthias squamipinnis*; Waite's splitfin, *Luzonichthys waitei* • Pixie Bommie, Great Barrier Reef • 8 metres

Basslets are well represented on parts of the reef that are exposed to currents. Along with damselfishes, they are one of the most abundant plankton-feeding fish groups on coral reefs.

38. Diver and pinnacle reef • Holmes Reef, Coral Sea • 20 metres • Fujichrome

In deeper lagoons, patch reefs often grow into vertical walled pinnacles towering as much as 50 metres or more above the sea floor. Their tops are generally a flattened plateau reaching the level of low tide.

39. Diver and reef flat • Ribbon Reef, Great Barrier Reef

This inner lagoon edge shelters a profusion of corals and in such locations permits delicate growth forms not possible in more exposed areas.

40. Corals and shark: *Acropora* dominated slope, Grey reef shark, *Carcharhinus amblyrhynchos*, 1.5 metres • Holmes Reef, Coral Sea • 15 metres • Fujichrome

The seaward edge of reefs is another focal point for life. Here there is an abundance of plankton feeders and patrolling predators. Coral growth is dense but assumes small, solid forms in response to strong wave motion.

41. Silhouetted divers • Ribbon Reef, Great Barrier Reef • 25 metres

Erosion and coral growth commonly combine to form vertical chimneys and caves along the outer face of reefs. Here a vertical chimney from the shallow reef top opens into a cave on the reef wall.

42. Reef reflection • Madang, Papua New Guinea • 2 metres • Fujichrome

In the upper part of the picture palm trees and other vegetation can be seen and below a critical angle, the reflection of the under surface and bottom of the reef is apparent.

43. Exposed reef • Flynn Reef, Great Barrier Reef

On the Great Barrier Reef tides range over several metres. On a few days each year unusually low tides can completely expose the tops of the reef for an hour or two. Exceptional calm and bright sun or rain at this critical time can kill the exposed corals.

44. Vegetated sand cay • Russell Islands, Solomon Islands • Fujichrome

45. Coconut sand cay • Madang, Papua New Guinea • Fujichrome

46. Island shoreline • Madang, Papua New Guinea • Fujichrome

47. Sand cay • Diamond Island, Coral Sea • Fujichrome

Reef islands support varying degrees of vegetation, from the classic desert island of pristine sand, to a dense cover of rainforest. Age, size, location, and rainfall influence the nature of life above the surface.

48. Island lagoon • Lord Howe Island, Australia

Lord Howe Island, 644 kilometres northeast of Sydney, Australia, lies at the southernmost limit of coral reefs. At this extreme, coral growth is limited and reef fauna includes a number of species that are unique to this area or rare elsewhere.

49 Left. Inner edge of a barrier reef • Ribbon Reef, Great Barrier Reef • Fujichrome

49 Right. Outer reef • Anderson Reef, Great Barrier Reef • Fujichrome

Views of the northern Great Barrier Reef. Deep passes bisect the reef and coral patches dot the sheltered lagoon behind. A white line of breakers denotes the outer seaward edge.

52. Red whip gorgonian, *Ellisella* sp. 80 cm • Holmes Reef, Coral Sea • 16 metres

Many of the attached animals of coral reefs have a plant-like appearance. The gorgonians or horny corals are related to the stony reef building corals but have a flexible skeleton of keratin which is similar to the material in animal horns and our own fingernails.

53. Harp gorgonian, *Ctenocella pectinata*, 80 cm • Whip gorgonian, *Juncella fragilis* • Lizard Island, Great Barrier Reef • 15 metres

There are hundreds of different species of gorgonians. They occur in a variety of forms including whips, harps, fans, and bushes that may be as large as three to four metres. In the West Indies large gorgonians are particularly abundant and their swaying motion lends a special ambience to those reefs.

54. Lavender gorgonian, probably *Acalycigorgia* sp. • Florida Group, Solomon Islands • 20 metres

55. Red gorgonian – unidentified • Bali, Indonesia • 20 metres

Gorgonians, like their relatives the stony corals, are colonial animals made up of numerous anemone-like polyps sharing a common skeleton. Gorgonian polyps are characterised by eight tentacles from which comes their scientific name, octocorals.

56. Yellow and red soft coral, *Siphonogorgia* sp. • Ribbon Reef, Great Barrier Reef • 20 metres • Kodachrome

This deep reef coral has an unusually soft sponge-like texture. Soft corals are still poorly studied and identification is often difficult.

57. Soft coral, *Dendronephthya* sp. • Lizard Island, Great Barrier Reef

Soft corals are another group of coral relatives. Unlike the stony and horny corals they have no continuous skeleton but instead have soft fleshy bodies in which tiny needle-like calcarious sclerites or spicules are embedded. The sclerites provide some support for the soft tissue and act as a deterrent to predators. In this species the polyps are red and the sclerites yellow.

58 Top. Black coral whip, *Cirrhipathes* sp. 1 m • Manus Island, Papua New Guinea • 15 metres

The black corals or anthipatharians are yet another group of coral relatives. They possess a dense tough skeleton that is extensively used for jewellery purposes. They are usually found at greater depths and can occur as both whips and branching trees.

58 Bottom. Miniature reef community: White encrusting sponge, poecilosclerid; Orange gorgonian, *Ellisella* sp.; white hydroids, yellow bryozoan; worm at bottom could be vermetid or spirorhid • Oyster Reef, Great Barrier Reef • 12 metres • Kodachrome

Sediment-free surfaces suitable for attached animals are at a premium in the sea and numerous organisms compete for such space where it is available.

59. Gorgonian, anemones and starfish: gorgonian – unidentified; anemone – unidentified; brittle starfish, *Ophiothrix purpurea* • Bali, Indonesia • 15 metres

The striped colonial sea anemone and brittle starfish are specialised inhabitants of certain gorgonians. This is a relationship that provides them with living space which is not utilised by other organisms.

60. Oyster community: Red and brown poecilosclerid sponges; Blue finger sponge, *Gelloides* sp.; soft coral at top, *Stereonephthya* sp.; grey soft coral, lower left, *Paralemnalia* sp.; black and yellow (also translucent) sea squirts; hydroids, algae, and brittle starfish • Michaelmas Reef, Great Barrier Reef • 12 metres • Fujichrome

Every corner of the reef is occupied by living things. This community shares a few square centimetres.

61. Leaf oysters: oyster, *Lopha folium*, 15 cm; poecilosclerid sponges • Michaelmas Reef, Great Barrier Reef • 12 metres

These are live oysters and the sponges are simply using the external surface of their shells for attachment.

62. Beehive coral, *Eleutherobia* sp., 3 cm • Michaelmas Reef, Great Barrier Reef • 12 metres

This small species of soft coral not only takes an unusual form but expands its polyps only after dark. Presumably it catches plankton rather than depending on plant cells in its tissue as do many gorgonians.

63. Soft coral, *Dendronephthya* sp., 40 cm • Rabaul, Papua New Guinea • 12 metres

When current is slack these soft corals collapse into a flaccid mass. However, when the current picks up, they inflate with water into an erect fan for feeding purposes. They come in an endless variety of colours and have a prickly feel.

64. Yellow feather starfish, *Comanthina nobilis*, 20 cm; encrusting sponge, *Nara nematifera* • Rabaul, Papua New Guinea • 8 metres

Crinoids or feather starfish are extremely ancient plankton-feeding life forms. Fossil crinoids similar to this one date back hundreds of millions of years.

65. Yellow brittle starfish, *Ophiothrix (Acanthophiothrix)* sp., 30 cm; crinoid – unidentified • Lizard Island, Great Barrier Reef • 15 metres

Brittle starfish or ophiuroids are named for their ability to voluntarily fragment, dropping arms if harassed. The black crinoid on which this individual was perched plays host to several different commensals but it is unclear in this case if the brittle starfish was a commensal or not.

66. Tubeworms, *Silogranella* sp., colony, 20 cm • Bali, Indonesia • 12 metres • Fujichrome

In most tubeworms their protective casing is buried in the substrate but this species has evolved to grow freely in a tree-like form. Perhaps they have evolved toxic or distasteful properties which permits them to live in this exposed manner.

67. Beachball sea cucumber, *Pseudocolochirus axiologus*, 30 cm • Green Island, Great Barrier Reef • 25 metres

Most sea cucumbers obtain their nourishment by ingesting bottom sediments but this species uses its tentacles to filter feed for plankton. When food is captured, the arms are inserted into the mouth, one after the other.

68. Feather duster worms, *Sabella* sp., 6 cm • Grand Cayman Island • 12 metres

The feathery appendages of these tubeworms are expanded to filter planktonic food. They can retract instantly into their leathery tubes if disturbed.

69. Christmas tree tubeworms, *Spirobranchus giganteus*, 3 cm • Madang, Papua New Guinea • 3 metres • Fujichrome

70. Tubeworm close-up, *Spirobranchus giganteus*, 3 cm • Pompey Reef, Great Barrier Reef • 5 metres

In this species, individuals exhibit a large variety of colour patterns. They have the ability to create burrows in the solid skeleton of stony corals. They secrete a sharp spike at the entrance which discourages small fish nipping at the delicate exposed gills which are also their filter feeding apparatus. This entire community can withdraw in an instant leaving a bare coral head. In close view, each animal can be seen to have two appendages plus an operculum, or door, which closes the burrow entrance when they retreat.

71. Red sea squirt, didemnid, 4 mm

72. Black spotter sea squirt, *Clavelina moluccensis*, 8 cm; blue sea squirt, *Rhopalaea crassa*, 10 mm • Bali, Indonesia • 12 metres • Fujichrome

73. Individual sea squirt, *Rhopalaea crassa*, 3 cm • Rabaul, Papua New Guinea • 10 metres

Tunicates derive their sustenance by filtering and some can extract micron size plankton from the water. They are sac-like animals that have two openings through which water passes in and out while feeding. In the close-up view, a network of blood vessels is obvious in the outer covering. Internally the pharyngial filtering mechanism is visible. The whole animal is enclosed in a layer of cellulose material known as the test. Some species are colonial and joined together by root-like connections.

76. Hingebeak shrimp, *Rhynchocinetes* sp., 6 cm • Thetford Reef, Great Barrier Reef

This species of hingebeak shrimp is apparently undescribed and new to science. This genus of shrimps gets its name from its unique hinged rostrum.

77. Hingebeak shrimp, *Rhynchocinetes vritai*. 4 cm • Lizard Island, Great Barrier Reef • 15 metres • Kodachrome

Unlike the previous species, this shrimp is active during the day and occurs in large groups, often running into the hundreds. These groups can form a dense carpet up to one metre across.

78 Top. Mantis shrimp, *Odontodactylus scyllarus*, 20 cm • Rabaul, Papua New Guinea • 8 metres

Mantis shrimps resemble a preying mantis in having large spiked raptorial claws and conspicuous compound eyes. They are active predators of other small reef creatures. Large specimens can pierce two centimetres of wood with their powerful claws.

78 Bottom. White saddled shrimp, *Thor amboinensis*, 1.5 cm • Phuket, Thailand • 6 metres

This small shrimp occurs right around the world on coral reefs. It is usually found in association with a variety of coelenterate hosts, mostly anemones. Like other anemone commensals, it exhibits a colour pattern of sharply defined white blotches.

79. Bumblebee shrimps, *Gnathophyllum americanum*, 1 cm • Bali, Indonesia • 4 metres • Kodachrome

Another tiny shrimp which has somehow found its way right around the world in the tropics. It usually occurs in pairs.

80. Harlequin shrimp, *Hymonocera elegans*, 5 cm • Mombasa, Kenya • 3 metres

This exotic shrimp usually lives in pairs and uses its specialised claws to cut open starfish on which it feeds. Its prey includes the coral-eating crown-of-thorns starfish.

81. Imperial shrimp, *Periclemenes imperator*, 2.5 cm; Holothurian, possibly *Euapta godeffroyi* • Lizard Island, Great Barrier Reef • 12 metres

The genus *Periclemenes* encompasses a number of species of small colourful shrimps that live as commensals with other reef creatures. This species usually lives in pairs with sea cucumbers or the Spanish dancer nudibranch.

82. Squat lobster, possibly *Galathea* sp., 1 cm • Bali, Indonesia • 20 metres • Fujichrome

The reef holds many secrets. This squat lobster, never before seen by the photographer, was recently found off Bali.

83. Skeleton shrimps, *Caprella* sp., 1 cm • Lizard Island, Great Barrier Reef

These unusual creatures are not true shrimps, but members of another group of crustacea, the amphipods. They are slender, small in size, and move in a distinctive manner, bringing the posterior of the body forward and arching the back, then moving the front part of the body forward in order to get a grip.

84. Zebra worm, *Baseodiscus mexicanus* • Sea of Cortez, Mexico • 12 metres

The zebra worm is an inhabitant of the Sea of Cortez commonly found at night when it emerges from its rocky daytime hiding place. When contracted, it can reduce to one-quarter of its expanded size of 80 centimetres.

85. Pipefish and sponge: Brown banded pipefish, *Corythoichthys amplexus*, 8 cm; sponge, poeciloscarid • Honiara, Solomon Islands • 4 metres

Pipefishes and their close relatives, seahorses, are encountered on, or very close to, the reef's surface. They are poor swimmers that rely both on their special armour of segmented bony rings and cryptic habits to discourage potential predators. Photographed at night.

86. Talpa cowrie, *Cypraea talpa*, 10 cm • Scooterboot Reef, Great Barrier Reef • 6 metres

The numerous species of cowries are among the most beautiful and popular of reef shells. The lustrous porcelain-like surface is maintained by the fleshy mantle which can be extended to completely envelop the shell. They are active nocturnal grazers.

87. Brindled cowrie, *Cypraea valentia*, 7 cm • Rabaul, Papua New Guinea • 35 metres

Until recently the brindled cowrie was among the rarest of shells to collectors and good specimens were in demand for as much as $2000. Few reef animals, however, are truly rare but many have habits and habitats that make them rarely encountered. Such was the case with this cowrie which has now been collected in some numbers, using new techniques at various localities. Photographed at night.

88. Ass's ear, *Haliotis asinina*, 10 cm • Lizard Island, Great Barrier Reef • 6 metres

Abalones are usually associated with temperate rocky areas but a few small species are found on tropical coral reefs.

89. Bubble shell, *Haminoea cymbalum*, 1 cm • Escape Reef, Great Barrier Reef • 1 metre

The bubble shell possesses a fragile shell completely enclosed in its fleshy body. This species lives under coral rubble on shallow reef flats.

90. Leafy sap slug, *Cyerce nigricans*, 2.5 cm • Escape Reef, Great Barrier Reef • 8 metres

91. Western Australian dorid, *Chromodoris* sp., 5 cm • Abrolhos Islands, Western Australia • 30 metres

92. Greenspot dorid, *Nembrotha kubaryana*, 5 cm • Lizard Island, Great Barrier Reef • 6 metres

93 Top. Lettuce leaf slug, *Tridachia crispatqa*, 7 cm • Grand Cayman Island • 12 metres

93 Bottom. Purple striped dorid, *Nembrotha purpureolineata*, 9 cm • Abrolhos Islands, Western Australia • 2 metres

Nudibranchs and sea slugs are molluscs that have replaced the protective armour of a shell in favour of toxic or distasteful chemical properties. Their bright colours make them readily identifiable and warn predators of their toxic nature. The name nudibranch means naked gill. In many species the gills protrude from the back as conspicuous bushy appendages.

94. Bigfin reef squid, *Sepioteuthis lessoniana*, 20 cm • Bali, Indonesia • 1 metre • Fujichrome

The cephalopods, squid, octopus, cuttlefish, and nautilus are among the most highly evolved invertebrates. They have a well-developed central nervous system, advanced eye, and their arms provide them with an unusual degree of manipulative ability. Photographed at night.

95. Chambered nautilus, *Nautilus pompilius*, 18 cm • Russell Islands, Solomon Islands

The chambered nautilus occurs at depths to several hundred metres in some areas of the Indo-West Pacific. They are a living fossil that were already ancient creatures before dinosaurs appeared, surviving virtually unchanged for hundreds of millions of years. This specimen was trapped at a depth of 200 metres and released in shallow water for photographic purposes.

96. Potato cod, *Epinephelus tukula*, 1 m • Cod Hole, Great Barrier Reef • 10 metres

One of the large groupers that is commonly encountered on Indo-Pacific reefs. It grows to a size of 1.5 metres and weighs at least 100 kilograms. Like other big groupers, these fishes are protandric hermaphrodites starting life as males and later changing sex to become females.

97 Top. Leaf scorpionfish, *Taenianotus triacanthus*, 8 cm • Flores, Indonesia • 10 metres

The leaf scorpionfish has variable colouration to blend in well with its surroundings. It is commonly seen in shades of red, yellow, brown, and black. It also has the unusual habit of periodically shedding its skin.

97 Bottom. Longhorn cowfish, *Lactoria cornuta*, 9 cm • Green Island, Great Barrier Reef • 2 metres

Cowfishes are bizarre creatures found on all tropical and subtropical reefs. They feed on a wide variety of benthic animals including tunicates, sponges, and alcyonarians. The rigid body armour of these fishes permits only the fins to move.

100. Radiolaria and dinoflagellates • Lizard Island, Great Barrier Reef • photo, P. Parks

These microscopic single-celled organisms are the basis for much of the food chain in tropical ocean and a source of sustenance for many filter-feeding reef animals.

101. Hyperiid amphipod, *Phronima* sp., 3 mm • Lizard Island, Great Barrier Reef

Phronima is a crustacean belonging to the oceanic amphipods. They live on and deposit their young within planktonic sea squirts. They dwell inside the bodies of their prey, invading them as juveniles and eating away tissue until only the barrel-shaped outer coat is left. The female raises her young within this home until the young amphipods are ready to leave, when it is thought she places them on another tunicate.

102. Porcellanid larvae, 8 mm • Lizard Island, Great Barrier Reef

Crustacea, like insects, develop through a series of distinct forms. The larvae of porcellanid crabs are readily identified by an exaggerated lance, or rostral spine, which later disappears. As an adult this creature becomes a normal crab.

103. Eel egg, 2 mm • Lizard Island, Great Barrier Reef

The early life of most reef fishes is spent drifting with the plankton. This embryo will develop into a transparent leaf-shaped larvae called a leptocephalus which may drift for weeks or months before settling on a reef and transforming into a conventional eel.

104. Crab zoea, 4 mm • Lizard Island, Great Barrier Reef

The zoea is an early stage in the larval development of many crustaceans. Unlikely as it may appear, this individual will eventually become a reef crab.

105. Hermit crab larvae, 4 mm • Lizard Island, Great Barrier Reef

A hermit crab in the early planktonic stage of its life. It will transform through a series of moults until it becomes a small adult. At this point it will settle out on a reef and seek an abandoned mollusc shell for a home.

106. Crab zoea, 5 mm • Lizard Island, Great Barrier Reef

The reproduction of reef creatures with planktonic larvae involves high mortality rates and thus the production of vast numbers of offspring.

107. Shrimp larvae, Penaeidae, *Gennadas*, 5 mm • Lizard Island, Great Barrier Reef

The spiky appendages of planktonic life forms probably provide some degree of defence against predation.

108. Amphipod, *Cyproidea* sp., 4 mm • Lizard Island, Great Barrier Reef

Planktonic crustaceans include not only the larvae of bottom-dwelling species, but also others that spend their entire lives in the ocean currents. Among the latter are many obscure groups about which little is known and identification is difficult.

109. Opal copepod, *Sapphirina* sp., 2 mm • Lizard Island, Great Barrier Reef

The iridescent colours of this male copepod are thought to serve as an attractant to the smaller females which live in association with salps (planktonic sea squirts).

110. Drifting siphonophores, *Porpita pacifico*, 4 cm • Lizard Island, Great Barrier Reef • photo, P. Parks

These surface-drifting siphonophores are actually colonies in which individual zooids radiate from a central float containing air chambers. They are related to the Portuguese man-o-war. Like much other plankton, these animals are not truly coral reef inhabitants but can be encountered drifting across reefs.

111. Planktonic nudibranch, *Glaucus atlanticus*, 2 cm • Gulf of Chiriqui, Panama

This planktonic nudibranch drifts in the open sea where it feeds on *Porpita* and related surface-drifting siphonophores.

112 Top. Comb jelly, *Beroe ovata*, 12 cm • Lizard Island, Great Barrier Reef • 2 metres

Comb jellyfishes are so transparent that often hundreds may be present without being noticed. This species is an envelope-shaped predator which readily engulfs other comb jellies as large as itself.

112 Bottom. Comb jelly, *Leucothea multicornis*, 12 cm • Lizard Island, Great Barrier Reef • 2 metres

Comb jellies or ctenophores possess tiny rows of fine comb-like appendages which break up light into the iridescent colours seen here. These can vary depending on viewing angle and incidence of light, creating a flickering fire effect.

113. Jellyfish, *Cephea cephea*, 50 cm • Similan Islands, Thailand • 1 metre

Jellyfishes are among the largest members of the drifting planktonic community. Juvenile fishes, particularly jacks, often accompany them, apparently immune to their stinging tentacles.

114 Top & Bottom. Cigar jelly, *Olindias phosphorica*, 6 cm Lizard Island, Great Barrier Reef

During the day this jellyfish retracts its tentacles and rolls up into a cigar shape. At night it unfurls a skirt of probing arms to capture food.

115. Plankton-feeding fishes: basslets, *Pseudanthias* and *Luzonichthys*; damselfishes (Pomacentridae); wrasses (Labridae) • Pixie Bommie, Great Barrier Reef • 3 metres

A virtual fish soup results in areas that combine strong currents and rich coral growth. The latter provides shelter for a myriad of small fishes that emerge to feed on plankton when the current is running.

116. Damselfishes and coral head: Bluegreen Chromis, *Chromis viridis*; coral, *Acropora cerealis* • Ribbon Reef, Great Barrier Reef • 5 metres

Small heads of branching corals often support huge numbers of damselfishes. They may range out a metre or more when actively feeding, but instantly retreat when approached by larger fishes. This behaviour can create the appearance of a pulsing aura surrounding the coral colony.

117. Orange ball anemone, *Pseudocorynactis caribbeorum*, 10 cm • Grand Cayman Island • 12 metres

The Caribbean orange ball corallimorph anemone is related to both corals and sea anemones. Their stinging capsules and internal anatomy are like those of corals, but they lack the calcarious skeletons of corals like sea anemones.

120. Snake eel, Ophichthyidae • Madang, Papua New Guinea • 20 metres • Fujichrome

Snake eels are well adapted for burrowing. The head is usually pointed and the tail is often tapered to a hard tip. These eels are adept at burrowing forwards or backwards. They are sometimes mistaken for sea snakes but are easily differentiated by their lack of scales.

121 Top & Bottom . Garden eels, *Gorgasia* sp. Holmes Reef, Coral Sea • 15 metres

Extensive colonies of garden eels are frequently seen on sandy slopes in deeper water. They may contain up to thousands of individuals which quickly retreat into the sand when approached. This species is as yet unnamed.

122. Tube anemone, cerianthid, 30 cm • Fitzroy Island, Great Barrier Reef • 15 metres

Tube anemones live in parchment-like cylindrical casings into which they can retreat if disturbed or threatened. Like other anemones their tentacles possess stinging cells which can paralyse their prey.

123. Tun shell, *Tonna perdix*, 15 cm • Bali, Indonesia • 10 metres • Fujichrome

The tun shell is a large mollusc that grazes the sand for food and is active mainly at night. It is capable of moving at a rate considered rapid for a large shelled mollusc.

124. Elegant sand diver, *Trichonotus elegans*, 17 cm • Rabaul, Papua New Guinea • 15 metres

Sand divers generally occur in aggregations consisting of numerous individuals. Much of their time is spent hiding under the sand with only the eyes and snout exposed. Mature males engage in spectacular displays possibly in competition for the available females.

125. Spinecheek goby, *Oplopomus oplopomus*, 8 cm • Rabaul, Papua New Guinea • 5 metres

There are hundreds of gobies inhabiting coral reefs, many are found only in sandy habitats. Most gobies are typified by the fusion of the pelvic fins into a disc-like apparatus.

126. Speckled grubfish, *Parapercis hexophthalma*, 15 cm • Diamond Islet, Coral Sea • 6 metres

Grubfishes frequent sand and rubble areas near coral reefs. All the species are carnivorous, feeding primarily on benthic crustaceans especially crabs and shrimps, although fishes may be taken. Some show slight colour differences between the sexes.

127. Elegant fire goby, *Nemateleotris decora*, 6 cm • Rabaul, Papua New Guinea • 20 metres

The fire gobies of the genus *Nemateleotris* are spectacular members of the reef community that occur mostly on outer slopes. They are usually seen in pairs that seem to communicate by flicking the antenna-like dorsal fin. When disturbed they retreat into a sandy burrow.

128. Schooling fishes: Sombre sweetlips, *Plectorhynchus schotaf*, 40 cm; Celebes sweetlips, *Plectorhynchus celebicus*, 40 cm; Gold-lined rabbitfish, *Siganus lineatus*, 30 cm • Green Island, Great Barrier Reef • 4 metres

Sweetlips occur worldwide in temperate and tropical seas. They resemble snappers but usually have a smaller mouth, thicker lips and lack enlarged canine teeth. They feed mainly on benthic invertebrates at night and shelter during the day.

129. Silver seapike, *Sphyraena helleri*, 45 cm • Holmes Reef, Coral Sea • 15 metres • Fujichrome

The barracuda family Sphryaenidae contains about 20 species distributed in tropical and subtropical seas. They are easily recognised by their characteristic shape and enlarged canine teeth. The diet consists mainly of fishes. Attacks on humans have been recorded in the Caribbean Sea.

130. Dash-dot goatfish, *Parupeneus barberinus*, 25 cm • Bali, Indonesia • 8 metres

Goatfishes use their barbels which possess taste organs to probe the bottom in search of food. They feed chiefly on crustaceans, worms, brittle stars, molluscs, heart urchins and small fishes. Other fish species occasionally follow close behind to take advantage of any organisms that may escape.

131. Lefteye flounder, Bothidae, 15 cm • Flores, Indonesia • 4 metres

Flounders have evolved camouflage and body form which enable them to lie flat and blend in with the sea floor. They begin life shaped more or less like ordinary fishes, but one eye gradually migrates to the opposite side of the head with increased growth. They are efficient predators of small fishes as evident in the photograph.

132. Green turtle, *Chelonia mydas*, 1 m

133. Raine Island, Great Barrier Reef

Raine Island, a tiny sand cay on Australia's Great Barrier Reef, may accommodate over 10,000 nesting green turtles per night at the height of the breeding season. They run a gauntlet of sharks which are attracted to the island at that time. Nests are so closely spaced that it is common for one to dig up the nest of another. The adult females may weigh over 100 kilograms and the effort to haul their bulk 100 metres or more over the sand is extreme. A few seem to lose their way and never make it back to the sea.

136 Top. Cleaner wrasse with sweetlips: Cleaner wrasse, *Labroides dimidiatus*, 7 cm; Painted sweetlips, *Diagramma pictum*, 50 cm • Lizard Island, Great Barrier Reef • 3 metres

Several types of cleaner wrasses are present on Indo-Pacific reefs. They perform an important function in the health of the fish community. A wide variety of fishes visit cleaning stations to have crustacean ectoparasites removed by these small wrasses. They also ingest mucus and dead wound tissue of the host fishes.

136 Bottom. Mimic blenny, *Aspidontus taeniatus*, 7 cm • Lizard Island, Great Barrier Reef

This species mimics the form, colour, and motion of the cleaner wrasse. This enables it to approach larger fishes in the guise of the true cleaner. It then uses its large sabre-like teeth to attack the soft tissue of the unsuspecting host. Their mimicry is so perfect that it is virtually undetectable and their activity in an area makes its victims wary of the genuine cleaner fish.
The mimic cleaner is not averse to attacking divers. If they were a metre in length instead of a fraction of that, Indo-Pacific reefs would be a dangerous place.

137. Weed whiting, *Siphonognathus attenuatus*, 12 cm • Busselton, Western Australia • 8 metres

The weed whitings are restricted to cool seas of southern Australia and New Zealand. They are close relatives of the wrasses, well adapted for life in weedy areas. The false eye spot is particularly effective for mis-directing predators amidst its weedy surroundings.

138. Black-saddled puffer, *Canthigaster valentini*, 6 cm • Euston Reef, Great Barrier Reef • 6 metres

Puffers very often have a powerful neurotoxin known as tetrodotoxin in their tissues, especially the liver and ovaries, which is capable of causing serious illness or death. In addition, they also have a repelling skin toxin and so are not bothered by predators.

139 Top. Mimic leatherjacket, *Paraluteres prionurus*, 5 cm • Norman Reef, Great Barrier Reef • 5 metres

The recognition of mimicry in wild animals was established by Henry Bates over a century ago. The basic components are the model (animal that is avoided for a valid reason) and the mimic or imitating animal. The less abundant and defenceless *Paraluteres* mimics the puffer because of the latter's toxicity.

139 Bottom. Footballer trout, *Plectropomus laevis*, 6 cm • Mahe, Seychelles• 8 metres

The previous two illustrations are examples of classical Batesian mimicry, but on reefs there are additional mimics that are involved in a single mimetic complex. The mimicry displayed by the footballer trout is not as precise as that of the filefish, nevertheless it affords some degree of protection particularly in the vulnerable juvenile stages.

140. Signal goby, *Signigobius biocellatus*, 5 cm • Opal Reef, Great Barrier Reef • 8 metres

Signal gobies generally occur singly or in pairs and are seen within a short distance of their burrow. They feed by gulping sand that is sieved through the gills, thus trapping small crustaceans, worms, etc. Predators mistake the ocelli and general side-on appearance of the goby for the head-on appearance of a larger fish.

141. Decoy scorpionfish, *Iracundus signifer*, 8 cm • Flic en Flac, Mauritius • 25 metres

Most scorpionfishes have effective camouflage colouration but this species has gone one step further. It utilises its fish-shaped dorsal fin to entice its victims. The decoy is so detailed that it includes a clearly visible eye, mouth, and fin outline. The only other fishes that employ a similar luring mechanism are the well-known anglerfishes.

142. Slender filefish, *Leprogaster tuckeri*, 2.5 cm • Grand Cayman Island • 10 metres

Filefishes, also known as leatherjackets are close relatives of the triggerfishes. However, unlike that group which display fixed colour patterns, many filefishes can alter their colouration to match their surroundings. This species takes the colour and pattern of its host gorgonian.

143. Prickly leatherjacket, *Chaetoderma penicilligera*, 8 cm • Bali, Indonesia • 5 metres

Many leatherjackets have highly mottled patterns in combination with filamentous appendages rendering them nearly invisible in weedy surroundings.

144. Crab with gorgonian: Spider crab, unidentified, 20 cm; gorgonian, *Plumigorgia* sp. • Michaelmas Reef, Great Barrier Reef • 6 metres

Certain spider crabs attach other reef organisms to themselves as camouflage. This one has disguised itself with a garden of gorgonians. Photographed at night.

145. Decorator crab, unidentified, 5 cm • Lizard Island, Great Barrier Reef • 1 metre • Kodachrome

Another spider crab camouflaged with the green calcarious algae *Halimeda* and sand grains.

146. Octopus, *Octopus tetricus*, 80 cm • Abrolhos Islands, Western Australia • 8 metres

The octopus uses both colour and shape to hide itself. Chromatophores or colour-bearing cells in its skin are under the control of its eye and nervous system and can instantly match the colour and pattern of its surroundings. In addition, they can raise fleshy appendages to match texture of their environment to complete a near perfect disguise.

147. Sargassumfish, *Histrio histrio*, 10 cm • Flores, Indonesia • 2 metres • Kodachrome

The sargassumfish is a member of an odd group commonly known as anglerfishes. They have a globular shape and their pelvic and pectoral fins have finger-like projections used for crawling-type locomotion. Their most interesting modification involves the first dorsal spine that is used as a luring apparatus and is tipped with an enticing bait. The latter is often like a worm or even in the shape of a small octopus. They also utilise colour and pattern to blend imperceptibly with their surroundings. This species is unusual in that it lives amid drifting sargassum weed at the ocean's surface.

148. Ghost pipefish and soft coral: Ghost pipefish, *Solenostomus paradoxus*, 12 cm; soft coral, *Dendronephthya* sp. • Rabaul, Papua New Guinea • 8 metres

Ghost pipefishes are closely related to normal pipefishes and seahorses. However, unlike them, the females assume the parental duties. The eggs are carried in a pouch-like structure formed by the partially fused pelvic fins. Ghost pipefishes are sometimes seen in open water, being conveyed by currents. Although entirely exposed, they are protected by their resemblance to floating weed and debris.

149. Leafy sea dragon, *Phycodurus eques*, 25 cm • Lucky Bay, Western Australia

The leafy sea dragon is unique to the south coast of Australia. It lives amongst kelp which it so closely resembles. It is actually a type of seahorse but males lack the typical brood pouch. Instead, the eggs are carried on the underside of the male's tail. Captive specimens have created a sensation in Japanese public aquaria in recent times.

152. Cowrie on soft coral: Allied cowrie, *Diminovula punctata*, 2 cm; Soft coral, *Dendronephthya* sp. • Hartley's Reef, Great Barrier Reef • 6 metres

A group of cowrie shells known as the allied cowries live in association with a variety of coral hosts and their colours and patterns match. These shells confuse the borderline between commensalism and parasitism. They graze on the tissues and perhaps secretions of their host but seem to do little or no damage.

153. Flamingo tongue cowrie, *Cyphoma gibbosum*, 3 cm • Grand Cayman Island • 6 metres

Found on a variety of gorgonian bushes and fans, this cowrie exhibits a variety of patterns and colour in its mantle. This is the common pattern. Strangely it does not match the colour of the host.

154. Imperial shrimps, *Periclimenes imperator*, 2 cm • Bali, Indonesia • 10 metres

Like other species of *Periclimenes*, the imperial shrimp pair differ in size with the male being noticeably smaller.

155. Spanish dancer nudibranch, *Hexabranchus sanquinensis*, 25 cm • Magnetic Island, Great Barrier Reef • 3 metres

The Spanish dancer is the largest nudibranch and can reach a length of over 30 centimetres. Normally they crawl on the bottom but also have the ability to swim freely. Their undulating swimming motion and colouration is reminiscent of the skirt of a flamenco dancer.

156. Needle shrimp, *Stegopontonia commensalis*, 2 cm • Bali, Indonesia • 2 metres • Fujichrome

The needle shrimp is a specialised commensal which lives only on the spines of the black-spined sea urchin, *Diadema*. It occurs in both the Indo-Pacific and Caribbean. Its unusual elongate form is accentuated by both its pattern of lengthwise white lines and its habit of holding its claws in close alignment with the body. Its legs are unusually short and adapted to grasping the thin needle spines of the urchin.

157   Top. Urchin with shrimps: Shrimp, *Periclimenes colemani*, 2 cm; Urchin, *Asthenosoma intermedium* • Low Isles, Great Barrier Reef • 12 metres

Another commensal *Periclimenes*. In this species the female is markedly larger than her mate. They are known only from the dangerous sea urchin *Asthenosoma intermedium*. The venom is not associated with the spines but is actually injected by small stalked flower-like appendages called pedicellariae. Although the toxin is powerful enough to be dangerous to humans, these tiny shrimp appear to enjoy a form of diplomatic immunity.

157   Bottom. Crab on urchin: Zebra crab, *Zebrida adamsi*, 1.5 cm; sea urchin, unidentified • Wentworth Reef, Great Barrier Reef • 15 metres

This species of eumedonid crab is a commensal on several species of urchins. Clearly visible on the hind legs are unusual grasping pincers adapted to holding the spines of the host.

158.   Squat lobster on crinoid: Elegant squat lobster, *Allogalathera elegans*, 2 cm; Feather starfish, *Comanthus bennetti* • Christmas Island, Indian Ocean • 10 metres

Found only in association with crinoids, the elegant squat lobster is in a group known as the galatheaids or half crabs. Like most commensals, this species has a colour pattern that blends with that of its host.

159   Top. Red shrimp on feather starfish: Pontoniine shrimp, *Paraportia nudirostris*, 2 cm; Feather starfish, *Himerometra robustipinna* • Wheeler Reef, Great Barrier Reef • 8 metres

Feather starfish have been prominent members of the coral reef community for hundreds of millions of years and have accumulated a number of specialised commensals including several species of shrimp.

159   Bottom. Yellow-spotted shrimp on feather starfish: Shrimp, *Synalpheus* sp., 3 cm; Feather starfish, *Comanthus parvicirrus* • Milln Reef, Great Barrier Reef • 12 metres

Most alpheids or snapping shrimps live independently in burrows that they construct. But a few, such as this species, have opted for life on or in other creatures.

160.   Shrimp and coral cod: Shrimp, *Lysmata amboinensis*, 7 cm;

Coral cod, *Cephalopholis miniatus* • Bali, Indonesia • 20 metres • Fujichrome

Certain types of shrimps offer the same service as the better known cleaner fishes. The shrimps establish cleaning stations in sheltered parts of the reef, often in caves or crevices. These locations are visited by fishes that require parasite removal. Shrimps that perform cleaning services possess conspicuous white antennae which they wave to attract host fishes.

161.   Shrimp and moray eel: Shrimp, *Lysmata amboinensis*, 7 cm; Vicious eel, *Gymnothorax breedeni* • Christmas Island, Indian Ocean • 30 metres

The aggressive reputation of moray eels is largely undeserved. Most are harmless and even the larger species hesitate to attack divers unless provoked. However, as its common name suggests, the vicious eel has a nasty disposition and will actively pursue and bite divers who enter their territory. This behaviour is not consistent though and may be associated with courtship activity.

162 & 163.   Anemonefish and host: Pink anemonefish, *Amphiprion perideraion*, 8 cm; anemone, *Heteractis magnifica* • Murray Island, Solomon Islands • 12 metres

The 28 species of anemonefishes are among the most colourful inhabitants of the reef. Some live with several types of anemones, but the pink anemonefish is host specific to *H. magnifica*, one of the largest host species. Its colour is variable, often blue, red, purple or brown. Anemonefishes usually occur in groups. The largest individual is a female, the next her mate, and the smaller individuals are juveniles whose development is retarded until something happens to one of the adults.

164.   Clown anemonefish, *Amphiprion percula*, 5 cm • Hastings Reef, Great Barrier Reef • 5 metres

Anemonefishes enjoy immunity from the tentacles of their host because of a special chemical in their external mucus, which prevents the stinging nematocysts from discharging. The immunity is acquired by newly settled juveniles after a brief acclimatisation period. This anemonefish species is perhaps the most colourful and best known.

165.   Spinecheek anemonefish, *Premnas biaculeatus*, 8 cm • Madang, Papua New Guinea • 10 metres • Fujichrome

Both anemones and fishes benefit from their commensal relationship. The protection of the fishes is obvious, but the advantage gained by the anemone is less apparent. The anemonefishes ward off tentacle-nipping fishes, remove debris from the tentacles, and are believed to promote the overall health of the host with their grooming behaviour. This unusual anemonefish is in its own genus, separate from others in the group.

166. Crabs on anemone: Porcelain crab, *Neopetrolisthes oshimai*, 2 cm; giant sea anemone, *Stichodactyla gigantea* • Russell Islands, Solomon Islands • 15 metres

This spotted crab lives with a variety of sea anemones. Tentacles of this anemone vibrate constantly and can be so adherent they pull off the anemone and stick to the hand. Commonly a male and female live with one host. Unlike the anemone shrimps, it is generally thought the largest of the pair is the male.

167 Top. Shrimp on anemone: Eggshell shrimp, *Periclimenes brevicarpalis*, 3 cm; adhesive anemone, *Cryptodendrum adhaesivum* • Rabaul, Papua New Guinea • 3 metres

As with other commensal species of Periclimenes this shrimp usually lives in pairs of which the male is noticeably smaller. They are also found on hard corals. The host in this photograph has two distinctive types of short, sticky tentacles. There is an outer band with a nodular shape and an inner area of slightly longer branching tentacles.

167 Bottom. Shrimp on coral: Appaloosa shrimp, *Periclimenes* sp., 3 cm; coral, *Euphyllia divisa* • Abrolhos Islands, Western Australia • 5 metres

Corals, like anemones, also have stinging tentacles which can afford similar protection to commensals.

168 Top. Crab and anemone: Harlequin crab, *Lissocarcinus orbicularis*, 4 cm; anemone unidentified • Bali, Indonesia • 15 metres • Fujichrome

This crab species is widespread in the Indo-Pacific and is usually found in association with sea cucumbers. This individual was living with a sand anemone and is holding a piece of the tentacle of its host, probably for defensive purposes.

168 Bottom. Boxer crab, *Lybia tessellata*, 2 cm • Bali, Indonesia • 4 metres • Kodachrome

Unlike other crustacean commensals, this little crab does not live on an anemone, but instead carries with it two complete small anemones. If attacked, the crab, like a boxer with gloves, spars one claw after the other in an endeavour to sting the opponent and thus deter it. The boxer crab is known to utilise at least three different species of anemones.

169. Trevally and jellyfish: Blue trevally, *Carangoides ferdau*, 18 cm; Rhizostome jellyfish, *Thysanostoma thysanura* • Rabaul, Papua New Guinea • 2 metres

Several species of trevallies are associated with pelagic jellyfishes during their juvenile stage. They enjoy the same sort of protection afforded anemonefishes by their hosts. The trevallies eventually outgrow their jellyfish companion, assuming an independent lifestyle.

170 Top. Goby, *Amblyeleotris* sp., 8 cm; shrimp, *Alpheus* sp. • Bali, Indonesia • 20 metres • Fujichrome

170 Bottom. Goby, *Amblyeleotris steinitzi*, 7 cm; shrimp, *Alpheus* sp. • Bali, Indonesia • 8 metres • Fujichrome

171 Top. Goby, *Cryptocentrus maudae*, 9 cm; shrimp, *Alpheus* sp. • Madang, Papua New Guinea • 3 metres • Fujichrome

171 Bottom. Goby, *Cryptocentrus cinctus*, 6 cm; shrimp, *Alpheus* sp. • Rabaul, Papua New Guinea • 5 metres

One of the most interesting commensal associations on the reef is that between gobies and alpheid shrimps. The shrimps' primary role is burrow maintenance. They constantly excavate their home, emerging periodically with a load of sand when the fish signals (with a flick of its tail) that it is safe. The fish serves as a sentinel, helping to co-ordinate the activities of the shrimp whose visual capabilities are limited. A lesser part of the relationship appears to be grooming activity on the part of the shrimp.

174 Top. Textile cone, *Conus textile*, 8 cm • Lizard Island, Great Barrier Reef • 1 metre

174 Bottom. Textile cone dart, 6 mm.

Cone shells are equipped with poisonous darts which are used to immobilise prey. Most species feed on small invertebrates and possess a toxin which is relatively harmless to humans. A few species, including the textile cone, however, have a venom which is toxic to vertebrates including man. Occasionally a would-be shell collector has been himself added to the collection of victims of these shells. The textile cone is equipped with a regenerating series of several dozen darts in progressive degrees of development.

175. Hermit crab, *Trizopaqurus strigatus*, 7 cm • Lizard Island, Great Barrier Reef • 10 metres

Hermit crabs have abandoned the usual body shell of crabs for the superior armour of molluscs.

176. Spotted porcupinefish, *Diodon hystrix*, 40 cm • Sea of Cortez, Mexico • 8 metres

Porcupinefishes are essentially puffers that are covered with spines. Normally the spines of *Diodon* lie flat, but when harassed by a predator or handled by a diver, the body is quickly inflated and the spines become erect.

177. Crown-of-thorns starfish and coral: Crown-of-thorns, *Acanthaster planci*, 45 cm; coral, *Favites complanata* • Tijou Reef, Great Barrier Reef • 8 metres

Like a number of other starfishes and their relatives the sea urchins, *Acanthaster planci* undergoes occasional population explosions. At such times, its coral devouring habits have made it notorious but there is no indication that this is other than a natural phenomenon. It even appears that it may play an important role in maintaining coral diversity on reefs by holding in check certain fast-growing species which are their preferred diet and which otherwise might dominate slower-growing forms. Studies on reef sediment cores on Australia's Great Barrier Reef have revealed fragments of *A. planci* skeletons in a pattern which indicates frequent population fluctuations going back tens of thousands of years.

178. Slate pencil urchin, *Heterocentrotus mammilatus*, 15 cm • Rabaul, Papua New Guinea • 10 metres

Sea urchins have made extensive use of spines for protection. These flattened spines on the underside of the slate pencil urchin surround its mouth. Those on the back are the size and shape of a pencil hence the common name.

179. Radiant star urchin, *Astropyga radiata*, 20 cm • Lizard Island, Great Barrier Reef • 15 metres

The rows of blue spots are light-sensing organs and reflect the pentaradiate symmetry of these creatures. The balloon-like structure in the centre of this photo is the anus which in sea urchins, is situated in the middle of the back.

180. Sabre squirrelfish, *Sargocentron spiniferum*, 40 cm • Pixie Bommie, Great Barrier Reef • 8 metres • Fujichrome

The squirrelfishes and soldierfishes of the family Holocentridae are cave-dwelling fishes by day and roving predators of small invertebrates by night. They are characterised by well-developed spination and even their scales are spiny. The large sharp spine on the cheek is mildly venomous and wounds from it may be extremely painful.

181. Lionfish and sponge: Ragged-finned lionfish, *Pterois antennata*, 15 cm; sponge, *Gelloides* sp. • Rabaul, Papua New Guinea • 10 metres

Scorpionfishes are amongst the most dangerous of the reefs inhabitants. All species contain toxic fin spines that are capable of inflicting painful wounds. These may vary in intensity from minor irritations, to coma, and even death. The lionfishes (also called firefishes) have grooved spines which deliver the venom. Treatment for such wounds is immersion in hot water.

182. Spotted boxfish, *Ostracion meleagris*, male, 10 cm • Christmas Island, Indian Ocean • 12 metres

Boxfishes produce a toxin known as ostracitoxin which is exuded when the fish is stressed. If a freshly collected boxfish is placed in a bucket or small aquarium with other fishes, they may die; if the concentration of the poison is strong enough it will also kill the boxfish.

183. Clown triggerfish, *Balistoides conspicillum*, 11 cm • Ribbon Reef, Great Barrier Reef • 20 metres

Distinctive warning colouration is sometimes used in conjunction with other defence mechanisms to warn away predators. The internal organs of the clown trigger are reputedly poisonous. It is one of the most highly prized aquarium fishes, fetching as much as $1000 when first introduced. Prices are now less than one-tenth of that. Initially it was considered rare, but it has since been found in numerous areas of the Indo-Pacific region.

184 Top. Flatworm, unidentified, 8 cm • Madang, Papua New Guinea • 12 metres • Fujichrome

Flatworms are unrelated to nudibranchs but similar in appearance and colouration. This probably serves the same warning purpose.

184 Bottom. Solar powered nudibranch, *Phyllodesmium longicirra*, 10 cm • Flores, Indonesia • 12 metres

This nudibranch has evolved an unusual form of defence. When aggravated it can discard some of its appendages or arms which float away and attach to the surroundings, focusing attention away from the body. These paddle-like appendages contain symbiotic zooxanthellae which may contribute partly to its nutritional needs. Other related nudibranchs have appendages in which they can store the undischarged stinging cells of coelenterates they feed on and thus utilise them for their own defence.

185. Pink dorid, *Chromodoris bullocki*, 7 cm • Bali, Indonesia • 8 metres • Fujichrome

The brilliant colours of nudibranchs are generally interpreted as warning colouration related to their distasteful properties.

186. Brownstripe seaperch, *Lutjanus vitta*, 18 cm • Michaelmas Reef, Great Barrier Reef • 10 metres

Schooling is a common mode of defence. A predator attacking a school of fishes finds it difficult to fix attention on any single individual. This confusion effect enables individuals to lose themselves among the mass. Confusion is often enhanced by colour patterns featuring repetitive stripes and dots which further serve to hide it amid the group.

187. Powder blue surgeonfish, *Acanthurus leucosternon*, 20 cm • Vilingilli, Maldives • 6 metres

Non-territorial grazing surgeonfishes like this species are exposed in their wanderings to both the aggression of territorial species and danger from predators in unsheltered places. Such species often travel in dense schools for defensive purposes. In addition to schooling, surgeonfishes have another potent defence, a scalpel-like apparatus on each side of the tail base. In species of *Acanthurus*, it is a pair of razor-sharp venomous blades that fold into a groove. These can be extended at right angles to the body and are a formidable weapon.

188. Blue sea star, *Linckia laevigata*, whole, 30 cm

189. Blue sea star, *Linckia laevigata*, regenerating, 5 cm • Briggs Reef, Great Barrier Reef • 8 metres

Many reef dwellers have an extraordinary ability to recover from extensive injury. Starfishes are a classic example and can regenerate the whole animal from a piece of one arm.

190. Portuguese man-o-war, *Physalia utriculus* • Lizard Island, Great Barrier Reef

The stinging tentacles of a Portuguese man-o-war are armed with some of the most potent stinging cells or nematacysts found in the sea. The nematacysts are common to corals, jellyfish, and related animals. They serve both in capturing prey and for defence. Despite the virulent stinging capabilities of the man-o-war, it is a favourite food of loggerhead turtles who appear to become temporarily intoxicated while feeding on them.

191. Tiger shark, *Galeocerdo cuvier*, 3.5 metres • Ribbon Reef, Great Barrier Reef • 5 metres

Perhaps the most feared shark in tropical seas is the tiger. It is reputed to grow to 5.5 metres and easily distinguished from other reef sharks by the blunt snout, vertical bars, and massive size of adults. The tiger shark gives birth to up to 50 live young. They normally feed on turtles, rays, and other sharks and a wide variety of lesser reef inhabitants. Their appetite is catholic and they have

been known to eat a deadly stonefish, bottles, tin cans, a ship's logbook, a wooden tom-tom, dogs, humans, and other flotsam and jetsam.

194. Spawning clams, *Tridacna gigas*, 1 metre • Escape Reef, Great Barrier Reef • 2 metres

Giant clams are fixed in one place. To successful reproduce they must synchronise their spawning with nearby individuals and produce massive quantities of gametes. The spawn acts as a pheremone which triggers others to spawn in a domino-like effect. Giant clams are the largest of shelled molluscs and may grow as large as 1.3 metres and weigh hundreds of kilograms.

195. Spawning urchin, *Tripneustes gratilla*, 11 cm • Rabaul, Papua New Guinea • 5 metres

A large part of the urchin's interior body structure is taken up by its reproductive organs. The ripe gonads of sea urchins are considered a gourmet food in some cultures. Photographed at night.

196. Spawning coral close-up, *Goniastrea* sp. eggs, 3 mm • Orpheus Island, Great Barrier Reef • 1 metre

197. Spawning corals –upper – *Acropora austera* eggs, 1 mm; lower – *Acropora hyacinthus* • Opal Reef, Great Barrier Reef • 3 metres

198. Coral eggs on surface • Escape Reef, Great Barrier Reef

Many reef corals produce conspicuous eggs during a brief annual spawning linked to the phase of the moon. At this time, the reef literally erupts in a mass orgy of spawning and a slow upward rain of eggs soon covers the surface of the sea with a pinkish blanket. The timing of this event, just before moonrise, maximises dispersal by currents while minimising predation by plankton-feeding fishes. The next morning vast windrows of eggs streak the sea surface inside the reef. On Australia's Great Barrier Reef, which has almost one-third of the world's coral, this phenomenon is so extensive that it shows up in satellite images. While most eggs are carried by currents from the reefs, the sea becomes so saturated that for a few days the water over the reefs is a rich egg soup. At this time many opportunist reef fishes abandon their normal feeding and hover above the reef gorging themselves on eggs.

199. Pederson's shrimp, *Periclimenes pedersoni*, 2 cm • Grand Cayman Island • 10 metres

Most crustaceans carry their eggs until they hatch into an early larval stage which drift away with the plankton.

200 Top. Slug-eating dorid, *Gymnodoris ceylonica*, 6 cm • Rabaul, Papua New Guinea • 2 metres

200 Bottom. Yellow nudibranch, *Notodoris minor*, 10 cm • Pellowe Reef, Great Barrier Reef • 10 metres

Nudibranchs lay gelatinous ribbons that contain their eggs. After they are deposited, the eggs are abandoned by the parent and develop on their own. The egg ribbons often match the colour of the parent and probably benefit from the same warning colouration.

201. Nudibranch, *Kentrodoris rubescens*, 10 cm • Bali, Indonesia • 20 metres • Fujichrome

202. Sea squirt colony: Sea squirts, *Didemnum molle*, 3 cm; encrusting sponge, *Nara nematifera* • Lizard Island, Great Barrier Reef • 8 metres

203. Sea squirt larvae, 5 mm • Lizard Island, Great Barrier Reef

Didemnum molle is a colonial ascidian with symbiotic algae. Each small hole along its sides is the inhalant siphon of a single zooid. The exhalant water is pumped out of the large hole at the top. The insides are covered with bright green algae. Free-swimming tadpole-type larvae are released from 11 am to 2 pm and are at first attracted to light. The larvae swims for about 20 minutes before it attaches to the substrate. It metamorphoses over about 10 minutes by retracting its tail and eventually takes the form of the barrel-shaped adult.

204. Cuttlefish eggs on sponges: eggs, 1.5 cm; sponges, both axinellids • Unity Reef, Great Barrier Reef • 3 metres

205. Cuttlefish, *Sepia latimanus*, 45 cm • Arlington Reef, Great Barrier Reef • 10 metres

Cuttlefishes and their relatives lay attached eggs, inside of which the young develop into miniature versions of the adult.

206 & 207. Thornback cowfish, *Lactoria fornasini*, 9 cm • Miyake-jima, Japan • 8 metres

When ready to spawn the male cowfish enters the female's territory and displays brilliant nuptial colours, at the same time rocking its body back and forth. The female responds by joining the male and swimming just in front of him. A slow deliberate spiral climb ends one metre below the surface when the fishes turn tail to tail, simultaneously releasing gametes (eggs and sperm). The pair then separate, retreating quickly to the bottom while the fertilised eggs drift away with the current. Spawning always occurs at sundown.

208. Gobies on seawhip: Goby, *Bryaninops loki*, 3 cm; seawhip, *Ellisella* sp. • Fitzroy Island, Great Barrier Reef • 12 metres

In contrast to many reef fishes that release pelagic eggs, the gobies lay demersal eggs which are firmly attached to the substrate. Seawhip gobies rotate around the whip attaching and fertilising their tiny eggs which are laid in exposed positions. During a short incubation period, the eggs are guarded by the parents. Many other gobies have concealed nests.

209. Eight-lined cardinalfish, *Cheilodipterus lineatus*, 12 cm • Flora Reef, Coral Sea • 8 metres • Fujichrome

Mouth brooding is a reproductive strategy utilised by few marine fishes. In cardinalfishes, a fertilised egg mass is taken into the mouth by the male and incubated for several days until hatching. During this period, he periodically juggles the egg mass and refrains from feeding.

210. Ornate pipefish, *Halicampus macrorhynchus*, adult, 10 cm • Rowley Shoals, Western Australia • 30 metres

Fishes that care for their developing eggs, such as pipefishes, have a high rate of hatching success in contrast to pelagic spawners who rely on vast egg numbers. Pipefish eggs are carried by the male on the ventral surface, either in a pouch or a specially vascularised surface. The newly hatched larvae have an enlarged yolk sac and are about four to five millimetres in length.

211. Japanese dragonet, *Neosynchiropus ijimai*, 7 cm • Miyake-jima, Japan • 12 metres

Dragonets are often characterised by differences in colour and fin shape between sexes. Males are more ornate and in many species the first dorsal fin is greatly enlarged and marked with eye-catching patterns. These features are used to attract females during courtship. Spawning takes place at dusk.

214. Parrotfish, *Scarus* sp., 35 cm • New Georgia, Solomon Islands • 10 metres

Parrotfishes often have two very different adult colour patterns. The first, termed the initial phase is generally drab dominated by dull reds and browns and is usually associated with females, but males may also be involved. The second, or terminal phase, is more colourful, dominated by bright greens and blues. This phase involves only males. The beaks of parrotfishes enable them to crunch the surface of coral rock to feed on algal stubble and boring algae within.

215. Splendid hawkfish, *Cirrhitus splendens*, 10 cm • Lord Howe

Island, Australia • 10 metres

At close distances small colour markings such as spots distinguish species but further away serve a disruptive function. Hawkfishes are small predators of crustaceans and fishes. Their common name is derived from the habit of perching on coral outcrops and surveying the immediate surroundings. The thickened lower pectoral rays are adapted for resting on the coral.

216. Golden Hamlet, *Hypoplectrus gummigutta*, 15 cm • Grand Cayman Island • 18 metres

The seven species of hamlets are almost identical in size and morphology but differ dramatically in their colour patterns. They are conspicuous members of the grouper family (Serranidae) on reefs in the tropical western Atlantic. They are functional hermaphrodites, capable of producing both eggs and sperm at the same time.

217. Lemonpeel angelfish, *Centropyge flavissimus*, 5 cm • Christmas Island, Indian Ocean • 10 metres

False eye spots may serve to misdirect attackers and can also be a distinctive feature for courtship and special recognition. Most pygmy angelfishes in the genus *Centropyge* show very little or no colour change during their development in contrast to other members of this family. However, the juvenile of this species is characterised by an ocellus which disappears as the fish grows.

218. Blue ribbon eel, *Rhinomuraena quaesita*, 80 cm • Christmas Island, Indian Ocean • 20 metres

This eel has three distinct colour phases. Black or blue with yellow margins and an overall yellowish phase. The dark phase are juveniles, blue are adult males and the yellowish phase are adult females. Their colourful nasal appendage may act as a lure for small fishes. They are popular aquarium fishes that become remarkably tame in captivity.

219. Dragon moray, *Enchelycore pardalis*, 70 cm • Miyake-jima, Japan • 5 metres

The dragon moray is an excellent example of disruptive colouration which does not follow the contours of the body and breaks up the appearance into unconnected parts. Most morays are nocturnal predators feeding mainly on fishes, occasionally on octopuses and crustaceans. They start life as males and later transform to females.

220. Harlequin sweetlips, *Plectorhynchus chaetodontoides*, 17 cm • Saxon Reef, Great Barrier Reef • 6 metres

The juvenile harlequin sweetlips is another prime example of confusion markings which break the body into unrecognisable fragments. Various species of sweetlips undergo dramatic colour changes with age. They generally have striking patterns of spots, stripes, or saddles when young. These gradually transform into the adult pattern which may be equally spectacular but dramatically different, or in some species a sombre grey or black.

221. Rockmover razorfish, *Novaculichthys taeniourus*, 7 cm • Elford Reef, Great Barrier Reef • 3 metres

Razorfishes are sand dwellers who compensate for the lack of shelter in their environment by turning sideways and diving into the loose sediments to escape predators. This juvenile sways with a motion-like moving weed. Adults lack the dorsal filaments and have a less cryptic pattern. Their common name is derived from the adult habit of shifting sizeable rocks with their jaws while searching for food.

222 Top. Coral cardinalfish, *Sphaeramia nematoptera*, 5 cm • Guadalcanal, Solomon Islands • 3 metres

The colour pattern of this species divides it into two visually unrelated halves. The cardinalfishes are one of the largest families of reef fishes. During the day they shelter, but roam widely after dark and are among the most abundant fishes seen on night dives. This particular species is encountered in large resting groups during the day amongst branching corals.

222 Bottom. Sailfin tang, *Zebrasoma veliferum*, 5 cm • Madang, Papua New Guinea • 4 metres

Deep-bodied reef fish often employ vertical bars and a dark band to hide the eye. The sailfin tang is usually solitary as a juvenile but forms pairs when mature.

223. Flame angelfish, *Centropyge loriculus*, 7 cm • Murray Island, Solomon Islands • 12 metres • Fujichrome

Distinctive colouration serves to advertise and identify territorial species such as the flame angel. This pygmy angelfish is unique in its brilliant red colour.

224. Orange-striped goby, *Amblygobius decussatus*, 8 cm • Bali, Indonesia • 10 metres • Fujichrome

Low contrast pastel markings permit close-up identification between fishes of the same species but are not obvious to distant predators. Gobies are the largest family of marine fishes with about 220 genera and 1600 species. They exhibit a wide variety of shapes, colours, behaviour, and habitat preferences. Gobies are among the most difficult fishes to identify because of their small size and the presence of many similar species.

225. Longnosed hawkfish, *Oxycirrhites typus*, 6 cm • Simbo Island, Solomon Islands • 20 metres • Kodachrome

The longnose hawkfish normally lives among the branches of gorgonians, black coral, and soft corals where the body pattern breaks up its appearance. It is usually found below a depth of about 20 metres and occurs widely throughout the Indo-Pacific region, east to the Americas.

226. Longnose filefish, *Oxymonocanthus longirostris*, 5 cm • Madang, Papua New Guinea • 1 metre • Fujichrome

During courtship and agonistic encounters, the male (shown here) fully extends its strikingly marked ventral flap. This fish uses its elongate snout to feed on live corals.

227. Whitetip soldierfish, *Myripristis vittata*, 13 cm • Christmas Island, Indian Ocean • 12 metres

At depths greater than six metres, red colours are not normally seen because red light is rapidly absorbed under water. At such depths red fishes appear simply as brown or grey. Predominantly red species which occur at shallow depths are usually nocturnal in habit like this soldierfish. Their diet consists mainly of larger planktonic crustaceans such as crab larvae.

228. Gilded triggerfish, *Xanthichthys auromarginatus*, 17 cm Christmas Island, Indian Ocean • 20 metres

Triggerfishes are among the most evolutionary advanced and have a large brain in relation to size. Unlike this species, most have similar colours in both males and females.

229 Top. Lined surgeonfish, *Acanthurus lineatus*, 28 cm • Christmas Island, Indian Ocean • 6 metres • Fujichrome

The lined surgeonfish is strongly territorial and maintains a private algal garden which it vigorously defends against any intruding grazers. The colourful pattern advertises its territorial claims.

229 Bottom. Orange-lined triggerfish, *Balistapus undulatus* 15 cm • Pixie Bommie, Great Barrier Reef • 6 metres

A special adaptation which give triggerfishes their name is a robust dorsal spike which can be locked in an erect position to avoid being swallowed or to wedge into crevices if threatened. Triggerfishes have a small mouth but powerful jaws and strong teeth. They are omnivores whose diet includes algae, plankton,

crabs, molluscs and sea urchins. They lay demersal eggs and these are aggressively defended by some of the larger species.

230 Top. Lyretail angelfish, *Genicanthus melanospilos*, 18 cm • Madang, Papua New Guinea • 20 metres • Fujichrome

Most angelfishes browse on attached reef organisms and have similarly coloured males and females. The lyretail angels, however, are unusual in that they are free swimming plankton feeders with elongate streamlined bodies and distinctively patterned males and females. They are deeper dwelling than other angelfishes and usually occur between 20 and 100 metres.

230 Bottom. Diagonal-banded sweetlips, *Plectorhinchus goldmani*, 45 cm • Bali, Indonesia • 3 metres • Fujichrome

Repetitive patterns of lines and dots though distinctive on isolated individuals, make them difficult to distinguish when they gather in a school which is the normal daytime habit of this species. The common name sweetlips is derived from their distinctive large fleshy lips. They are members of the family Haemulidae that occurs worldwide in tropical seas but the genus *Plectorhinchus* is restricted to the Indo-Pacific region. The flesh of larger sweetlips is good eating.

231. Wheeler's shrimp goby, *Amblyeleotris wheeleri*, 5 cm • Bali, Indonesia • 6 metres

From a few metres away in its natural environment where red is filtered out and fine detail diffused, the brilliant colours of this fish are not apparent. Under such conditions, its form is disrupted by dusky bands and it becomes inconspicuous. Up close the fine markings serve a role in courtship and species recognition.

232. Royal Gramma, *Gramma loreto*, 6 cm • Grand Cayman Island • 15 metres

The colours of the Royal Gramma from the Caribbean are obviously designed to advertise, not conceal. In the Pacific Ocean a similar pattern has independently evolved in the dottyback family.

233. Bicolor parrotfish, *Cetoscarus bicolor*, 6 cm • Moore Reef, Great Barrier Reef • 8 metres

This species has a unique juvenile colour phase and is solitary. Most other parrotfishes have drab juvenile patterns of brown with cream stripes and are schooling. Later in life this and other juvenile patterns are replaced by an initial adult colour phase which, in some, may change dramatically again to a terminal male phase. For many years the distinctively different colour of juvenile and adult and male and female parrotfishes led early ichthyologists to believe that each was a separate species. In recent decades diving scientists observing consistent associations and intermediate colour stages have been able to correctly place the differing patterns into the appropriate species.

234 Top. Lyretail wrasse, *Bodianus anthioides*, 8 cm • Shimoni, Kenya • 15 metres

The lyretail wrasse, unlike other members of the family, has evolved the body form, colour, and feeding habits of successful plankton eaters. Juveniles sometime engage in parasite cleaning of larger fishes. However, a number of diverse species also serve as fish cleaners including certain other wrasses and butterflyfishes.

234 Bottom. Splendid dottyback, *Pseudochromis splendens*, 8 cm • Flores, Indonesia • 20 metres • Fujichrome

This dottyback combines stripes, spots, distinctive fin margins, and an eyeband in a striking combination of features. Dottybacks are small, often colourful fishes that are cryptic inhabitants of crevices and ledges. Female to male sex reversal appears to be common. The female deposits a ball of eggs that sticks to the bottom. It is guarded by the male who sometimes moves its position by picking up the mass in its mouth.

235 Top. Dwarf hawkfish, *Cirrhitichthys falco*, 6 cm • Bali, Indonesia • 10 metres

235 Centre. Banded hawkfish, *Cirrhitops fasciatus*, 7 cm • Coin-de-mer, Mauritius • 20 metres

235 Bottom. Arc-eye hawkfish, *Paracirrhites arcatus*, 6 cm • Christmas Island, Indian Ocean • 12 metres

The apparently brilliant colours of these hawkfishes are the result of the photographer's flash. In nature they present a drab appearance which blends into the background. The hawkfishes include 35 species in 10 genera which occur mainly in the tropical Indo-Pacific region. One of their diagnostic features is the presence of several short tassel-like filaments (cirri) on the tips of the dorsal spines and on the anterior nostrils. They are lurking predators, feeding mainly on unwary small fishes and crustaceans.

236. Linespot wrasse, *Paracheilinus lineopunctatus*, 7 cm • Batangas, Philippines • 12 metres

The colourful *Paracheilinus* wrasses form aggregations that feed on zooplankton a short distance above the bottom. Males are more colourful and generally larger in size than females. Males preside over a harem; during courtship they display a brilliant

intensification of colour accompanied by the erection of their distinctive dorsal fin.

237. Cheeklined maori wrasse, *Cheilinus diagrammus*, 20 cm • Yonge Reef, Great Barrier Reef • 8 metres

Wrasses are among the most abundant and speciose of reef fishes. Most are brightly coloured and often the juveniles, females and males have entirely different colour patterns. Sex reversal occurs in many species; they begin adulthood as females but later change sex. Along with a change of sex, many species assume a more brilliant male colour pattern.

238. Mandarin fish, *Synchiropus splendidus*, 4 cm • Haggerstone Island, Great Barrier Reef • 3 metres

Highly territorial species like the mandarin fish are among the most brilliantly patterned of reef fishes. Like other dragonets, it also has a spectacular dorsal fin which it can display to add to its impact. They are generally small fishes, often under 10 centimetres, that dwell on reefs and in sandy or rubble areas. The mandarin fish has a curious hopping type of locomotion that involves slow crawling movements alternating with short swimming bursts, always close to the bottom.

239. Blue tang, *Paracanthurus hepatus*, 10 cm • Carter Reef, Great Barrier Reef • 2 metres

Plankton feeders who move up into the water column are often coloured blue. Most surgeonfishes are algal feeders but this species and a few others consume mainly plankton. This surgeonfish occurs widely but not abundantly on Indo-Pacific coral reefs and is a shy species that flees or takes shelter amongst branching coral at the approach of a diver.

240. Long-finned batfish, *Platax pinnatus*, 7 cm • Florida Group, Solomon Islands • 3 metres

The juvenile long-finned batfish is extraordinary in both form and colour. When very young its appearance and movement closely resemble a toxic polyclad flatworm, thus affording a degree of freedom from predation. Juvenile batfishes are very popular with aquarists and the adults frequently occur in schools and seem to be attracted to divers.

241. Harlequin tuskfish, *Choerodon fasciatus*, 15 cm • Sudbury Reef, Great Barrier Reef • 5 metres • Fujichrome

The dentition of wrasses is often indicative of their life style. The well-developed canine-like teeth of the tuskfishes belonging to the genus *Choerodon* are handy for turning over stones while foraging, and for crushing molluscs, an important part of their diet.

244   Top. Saddled butterflyfish, *Chaetodon ephippium*, 17 cm • Jewell Reef, Great Barrier Reef • 5 metres

244   Bottom. Racoon butterflyfish, *Chaetodon lunula*, 16 cm • Bali, Indonesia • 3 metres • Kodachrome

245.   Copperband butterflyfish, *Chelmon rostratus*, 10 cm • Lizard Island, Great Barrier Reef • 2 metres

Among the 116 species of butterflyfishes, body form and size are similar. However, the species differ markedly in colour pattern. They are amongst the most conspicuous and colourful of reef inhabitants. Most species generally occur in pairs, are territorial and restricted to a small area of the reef. They constantly move about foraging for food. Many feed exclusively on live corals, others consume a mixed diet consisting of small benthic invertebrates and algae. A few species, for example members of *Hemitaurichthys*, feed on zooplankton in midwater.

246.   Regal angelfish, *Pygoplites diacanthus*, 16 cm • Milln Reef, Great Barrier Reef • 10 metres

247.   Blue-girdled angelfish, *Pomacanthus navarchus*, 17 cm • New Georgia, Solomon Islands • 12 metres • Fujichrome.

248.   Queen angelfish, *Holocanthus ciliaris*, 30 cm • Grand Cayman Island • 12 metres

249.   Yellow-faced angelfish, *Pomacanthus xanthometopon*, 30 cm • Bali, Indonesia • 12 metres • Fujichrome

250.   Scribbled angelfish, *Chaetodontoplus duboulayi*, 20 cm • Low Isles, Great Barrier Reef • 15 metres • Kodachrome

251.   Conspicuous angelfish, *Chaetodontoplus conspicillatus*, 16 cm • Lord Howe Island, Australia • 12 metres

Angelfishes like their smaller relatives the butterflyfishes, have exploited a successful body style to evolutionary diverge into a variety of species distinguished chiefly by spectacular colour patterns. They differ from the butterflyfishes in being generally larger and in possessing a sabre-like spine on the cheek. They are dependent on shelter in the form of boulders, caves and coral crevices. Typically, they are territorial, spending daylight hours near the bottom in search of food. Their diet varies according to species. Some feed almost entirely on algae, others eat a variety of benthic invertebrates including sponges. The latter is a feat achieved by few other fishes. Protected by spicules and toxins, sponges are the dietary equivalent of ground glass with poison. A few angelfishes, the lyretails, have become midwater zo-

oplankton feeders. Large adults of the genus *Pomacanthus* sometimes startle divers with a powerful grunting sound. There are 75 species of angelfishes worldwide.

252.   Blue devil, *Chrysiptera cyanea*, 6 cm • Madang, Papua New Guinea • 1 metre • Fujichrome

253   Left. Goldtail demoiselle, *Chrysiptera parasema*, 4 cm • Madang, Papua New Guinea • 5 metres • Fujichrome

253   Right. South seas devil, *Chrysiptera taupou*, 6 cm • Herald Cays, Coral Sea • 4 metres • Fujichrome

254   Top. Javanese damsel, *Paraglyphidodon oxyodon*, 3 cm • Flores, Indonesia • 2 metres

254   Bottom. Cross's damsel, *Paraglyphidodon* sp., 3 cm • Flores, Indonesia • 2 metres

255.   Multispine damselfish, *Paraglyphidodon polyacanthus*, 4 cm • Lord Howe Island, Australia • 6 metres

Like other poster-coloured territorial reef fishes, damselfishes tend to be aggressive defenders of their chosen space and often successfully drive away intruders many times their own size. They are highly visible in virtually all reef habitats. There are 320 species among 28 genera in the family. Most are similar in body shape and size but many species, like the butterfly and angelfishes, exhibit distinctive colouration.

Damsels exhibit a wide range of feeding habits. Species which feed largely on algae are very often drab coloured, whereas the more colourful forms such as those shown here, consume a mixed diet that include benthic invertebrates and plankton. Reproductive behaviour is highly stereotyped and most often involves a single male spawning with one or more females after a prenuptial bout of nest preparation and courtship displays. The eggs are laid on the bottom and subsequently guarded by the male parent. Hatching occurs in about three to seven days and the larvae are pelagic for variable periods of seven to 50 days, depending on the species.

256.   Redfin basslet, *Pseudanthias dispar*, 6 cm • Lena Reef, Great Barrier Reef • 8 metres • Fujichrome

257   Top. Stocky basslet, *Pseudanthias hypselosoma*, 7 cm • Mactan Island, Philippines • 12 metres

257   Bottom. Redbar basslet, *Pseudanthias rubizonatus*, 8 cm • Lady Elliott Island, Great Barrier Reef • 15 metres

258.   Scalefin basslet, *Pseudanthias squamipinnis*, 7 cm • Madang, Papua New Guinea • 12 metres

259   Top. Cave basslet, *Serranocirrhitus latus*, 7 cm • Lihou Reef,

Coral Sea • 10 metres

259 Bottom. Threadfin basslet, *Pseudanthias huchtii*, 7 cm • Rabaul, Papua New Guinea • 6 metres • Fujichrome

260. Purple basslet, *Pseudanthias tuka*, 8 cm • Euston Reef, Great Barrier Reef • 6 metres • Kodachrome

261. Pink and yellow basslet, *Nemanthias carburyi*, 8 cm • Vilingilli, Maldives • 8 metres

In most large families of reef fishes certain species have abandoned a bottom-living mode and have evolved a form that is modified for midwater feeding. Their special adaptations include a more elongate body form, forked tail, small terminal mouth, small teeth, and forward looking eyes that provide close-up binocular vision. These brightly coloured basslets of the grouper subfamily Anthiinae are a good example of this phenomenon. They are a conspicuous part of the outer reef slope fish community, forming colourful shimmering shoals.

262 Top. Squarespot basslet, male, *Pseudanthias pleurotaenia*, 10 cm • Bali, Indonesia • 35 metres • Kodachrome

262 Bottom. Squarespot basslet, female, *Pseudanthias pleurotaenia*, 9 cm • Bougainville Reef, Coral Sea • 25 metres

263. Squarespot basslet, males, *Pseudanthias pleurotaenia*, 10 cm • Bali, Indonesia • 35 metres • Fujichrome

264. Twinspot basslet, female, *Pseudanthias bimaculatus*, 9 cm • Bali, Indonesia • 40 metres • Kodachrome

265. Twinspot basslet, male, *Pseudanthias bimaculatus*, 10 cm • Bali, Indonesia • 40 metres • Fujichrome

Basslets and several other groups of reef fishes are capable of sex reversal and have a harem social structure consisting of a single male with a number of females. If the male is killed or experimentally removed, the dominant female develops functioning testes and the more colourful male pattern. At the depth that the pictured species live, the yellow colouration of the females appears as in the photographs. However, the red of the males is not evident and appears as pale blue with dark blue markings. The genus *Pseudanthias* is restricted to Indo-Pacific reefs.

266. Emperor angelfish, adult, *Pomacanthus imperator*, 30 cm • Flores, Indonesia • 15 metres • Fujichrome

267. Emperor angelfish, juvenile, *Pomacanthus imperator*, 7 cm • Bali, Indonesia • 15 metres • Fujichrome

268. King angelfish, adult, *Holocanthus passer*, 28 cm • Sea of Cortez, Mexico • 12 metres

269. King angelfish, juvenile, *Holocanthus passer*, 8 cm • Sea of Cortez, Mexico • 12 metres

Difference in size between juveniles and adults of some reef fishes, imposes differences in food, predators, competitors and habitat. This is often accompanied by distinctive contrasts in the colour patterns between young and old. Some are so different that early ichthyologists mistakenly described them as separate species.

Angelfishes of the genera *Holocanthus* and *Pomacanthus* exhibit such dramatic colour differences. The patterns of the young consist of pale bars or irregular concentric rings which are vividly contrasted against a dark background. Such patterns appear to produce a dazzle effect. Combined with the dark stripe hiding the eye, they may serve to confuse or misdirect the attack of other small territorial reef fishes.

272 Top. Goby, *Cryptocentrus* sp., 10 cm • Rabaul, Papua New Guinea • 8 metres

272 Bottom. Goby, *Vanderhorstia* sp., 5 cm • Laing Island, Papua New Guinea • 8 metres

273 Top. Goby, *Amblyeleotris* sp., 8 cm • Rabaul, Papua New Guinea • 10 metres

273 Bottom. Goby, *Oxyurichthys* sp., 7 cm • Rabaul, Papua New Guinea • 17 metres

Ichthyologists estimate that there are between 20,000 to 25,000 species of fishes and new discoveries are still frequently being made. A particularly fertile source in this respect is the family Gobiidae. Many have escaped detection because of their cryptic habits and affinity for unattractive environments, including turbid silt bottoms, sand flats, etcetera.

274. Randall's shrimp goby, *Amblyeleotris randalli*, 8 cm • Flores, Indonesia • 12 metres • Fujichrome

This shrimp goby was first discovered on the island of New Britain, Papua New Guinea. It has since been found at other localities including Indonesia and the Philippines. It occurs on steep outer slopes at depths below 10 metres.

275. Longfin basslet, male, *Pseudanthias ventralis*, 5 cm • Holmes Reef, Coral Sea • 55 metres

Many of the newly discovered reef fishes which have been described over the past three decades are species that are restricted to steep outer reef slopes below 20 metres. The widespread use of scuba apparatus has enabled diving scientists to probe this previously unsampled region. The longfin basslet lives between 40-60 metres. It is one of a multitude of species discovered and named by Dr John E. Randall who first found it at Pitcairn Island, the isolated home of the *Bounty* mutineers.

276. Randall's basslet, male, *Pseudanthias randalli*, 6 cm • Bali, Indonesia • 30 metres • Fujichrome

The muted hues of the deep reef are transformed into a vibrant palette of colours with artificial light. For example, under natural conditions, Randall's basslet appears to be a mix of dull browns and greys. But when illuminated, these colours are magically transformed into dazzling violet, red and magenta.

277. Bluehead tilefish, *Hoplolatilus starcki*, 12 cm • Madang, Papua New Guinea • 29 metres • Fujichrome

This species was first found at Enewetak Atoll and subsequently at widespread locations in the western Pacific. It feeds on plankton and hovers up to five metres or more above the bottom but descends and dives into burrows if approached. Normally they are found on deep outer reef slopes below 20 metres.

The genus *Hoplolatilus* contains eight other species. They are confined to Indo-Pacific reefs and because of their relatively deep dwelling and burrowing habits, these fishes are not often observed by divers. Until the 1970s only two species were known but scuba diving scientists have since contributed greatly to the knowledge of this group. The most recent find was *H. luteus* collected from 30 metres on Indonesian reefs in 1988.

278. Filament wrasse, *Paracheilinus filamentosus*, 6 cm • Rabaul, Papua New Guinea • 18 metres

279. McCosker's filament wrasse, *Paracheilinus mccoskeri*, 5 cm • Bali, Indonesia • 12 metres

The genus *Paracheilinus* contains seven species that range from the Red Sea and Madagascar to Melanesia. The first species was described from the Red Sea in 1955, all others were discovered between 1973 and 1978. The individuals featured are both males in courtship display. During this display they erect their elongate fins and perform a dance and their colour pattern is momentarily intensified. The intensification is such as to produce a neon-like effect.

280 & 281. Merlet's scorpionfish, *Rhinopias aphanes*, 15 cm • Flynn Reef, Great Barrier Reef • 9 metres • Kodachrome

This rare fish is one of the most exotically camouflaged of scorpionfishes. Known from only a handful of specimens found in the Coral Sea region, it is highly prized in the aquarium trade and can command a price of up to $2000. Like other members of the family they have venomous spines. *Rhinopias* also has the ability to shed its skin.

282. Scarlet shrimp, *Lysmata debelius*, 4 cm • Bali, Indonesia • Fujichrome

283. Violet-spotted reef lobster, *Enoplometopus debelius*, 6 cm • Bali, Indonesia • Fujichrome

Both the scarlet shrimp and violet-spotted reef lobster are recent discoveries named for the German photo-journalist Helmut Debelius, who first brought them to the attention of scientists.

284. Red sea cucumber, *Thelenota* sp., 40 cm • Rabaul, Papua New Guinea • 12 metres

This soft-thorned sea cucumber has been seen at various localities in the western Pacific. It still lacks a scientific description and name. Photographed at night.

285. Reef shrimp, unidentified • Bali, Indonesia • 12 metres • Fujichrome

Reef shrimps occur in an endless variety of forms. This individual represents a species of pontoniine or palaemonine shrimp as yet unknown to science. In an effort to obtain an unobstructed photograph, it was chased on to a sea urchin which may not be its normal habitat.

288. Man-made islands • Lau Lagoon, Solomon Islands • photo, J. Tobin

Reef villages in Lau Lagoon, Solomon Islands. Around the mountainous island of Malaita, coastal peoples have constructed man-made islands from coral debris. Reef dwellings afforded them protection from attack and easy access to their food source.

289. Skull cairn • Kundu Island, Solomon Islands • Fujichrome

In the Solomon Islands a canoe prow shelters the skulls of important ancestors and their clam-shell wealth. Such shrines are a residing place for the spirits. The rings, or *bahika*, were their most important items of wealth. They were made from ancient giant clams found in forest areas where reefs have been upthrust by geological activity.

290. Reef tourist facility • Norman Reef, Great Barrier Reef • Fujichrome

A large-scale tourist operation. High speed catamarans capable of carrying several hundred visitors make daily excursions to Australia's Great Barrier Reef.

291. Magic carpet ride • Ribbon Reef, Great Barrier Reef

A ride across the reef on a glass-calm day affords a unique

perspective of the extraordinary spectacle passing beneath.

292. Diver with moray eel; Moray eel, *Gymnothorax javanicus* • Cod Hole, Great Barrier Reef • 8 metres • Fujichrome

293 Top. Diver and soft coral: Soft coral, *Dendronephthya* sp.; branching whips, *Ellisella* sp. • Holmes Reef, Coral Sea • 12 metres • Fujichrome

293 Bottom. Diver and small fish: Schooling sweeps, *Parapriacanthus* sp.; Black fish, *Dascyllus trimaculatus*; Anemonefish, *Amphiprion melanopus* • Holmes Reef, Coral Sea • 6 metres

Coral reefs have become a mecca for divers. The irresistible attraction of their beauty has fostered the development of diving tourism at exotic locations all over the world. Scuba diving on reefs is one of the ultimate human experiences of nature. A teeming abundance of diverse, spectacular, and approachable life provides an intimate close-up experience beyond that available anywhere else. The diver with the moray eel is Oren Dickason from the U.S.A., still actively diving and seeking underwater adventures at age 76.

294. Suspended divers • Ribbon Reef, Great Barrier Reef • 12 metres

295. Diver on reef edge • Black Rock Reef, Great Barrier Reef • 12 metres

Weightlessly suspended by luminous blue water, divers are free to explore the reef in all three dimensions. Gliding slowly across the coral, effortlessly ascending towering vertical walls and plunging silently into the depths, they have access to the reef and all its realms.

296 & 297. Divers and potato cod; Potato cod, *Epinephelus tukula*, (1-1.5 metres) • Cod Hole, Great Barrier Reef • 8 metres

The potato cod ranges widely from East Africa to Polynesia. It is usually solitary in habit and only seen occasionally by divers. However, at several localities on Australia's Great Barrier Reef, these giants of the reef are found in numbers. At the well-known Cod Hole, near Lizard Island they are a premier tourist attraction being hand-fed regularly.

298. Divers in sunbeam • Bailey's Custom Cave, Solomon Islands

299. Silhouette in cave • Christmas Island, Indian Ocean

Sunlight beaming through a hole in the roof of a cave on a South Pacific island creates a cathedral-like effect. At Christmas Island in the Indian Ocean a diver explores a large shoreline cave eroded by wave action.

Caves and grottos are common features of island shorelines and reef walls. They provide a special environment inhabited by unusual creatures and offer divers a further unique reef experience.

300. Diver near island • Madang, Papua New Guinea • Fujichrome

Tropical islands can offer immediate sheltered access to reefs amid idyllic surroundings.

301. Tracked vehicle • Russell Islands, Solomon Islands • 12 metres

302. Army jeep • Russell Islands, Solomon Islands • 20 metres

303. Truck • Russell Islands, Solomon Islands • 25 metres

304. Float plane • Rabaul, Papua New Guinea • 20 metres

305. Jungle tank • Gizo, Solomon Islands • 20 metres

306. Fighter • New Georgia, Solomon Islands • 12 metres

307. Gun turret • Guadalcanal, Solomon Islands • 10 metres

Throughout the western Pacific the debris of the Second World War has added an interesting dimension of recent human history to the reef. On land, such wreckage remains a rusting eyesore, but in the sea it is quickly claimed for living space by exotic reef organisms blending it into the natural seascape.

Although the horrors of war have long since passed, danger can still lurk in such seemingly tranquil settings. Soon after the truck was photographed at West White beach in the Russell Islands, there were two separate fatal attacks on swimmers by a large crocodile.

334. Pike blenny, *Chaenopsis schmitti*, 8 cm • Isla Rabida, Galapagos • 8 metres

The pike blenny is a fascinating reef inhabitant that occurs in the tropical Eastern Pacific and Atlantic oceans. These elongate fishes occupy vacant worm tubes situated on featureless sand bottoms. The male has a sail-like dorsal fin which it erects to attract the female. This display is greatly enhanced by its orange throat.

335 & 336. Redlip batfish, *Ogcocephalus darwini*, 15 cm • Isla Fernandina, Galapagos • 12 metres

This species is unrelated to the Indo-West Pacific *Platax* which are also known as batfishes. It is actually a relative of the anglerfishes having a luring device to attract small prey. It occurs in sandy areas below 12 metres, remaining motionless on the bottom for long periods of time.

Photographic Details

Most of the photos appearing in this book were taken with Ektachrome film, however, in recent times I have changed to Fujichrome. For readers interested in comparisons, the Fujichromes and a few Kodachromes are mentioned in the Commentary

I use a Nikon F2 camera with action finder and 24 mm, 55 mm macro and 105 mm macro lenses. The half-in half-out photos were taken with a 20 mm lens utilising one-half plus three diopter for beneath the water and a one-half polarising filter for above. A large port made from a compass dome was used for this purpose. The natural light wide angles were shot with a Nikonos III with 15 mm lens. The plankton photos were taken with a Wild M400 photo-microscope and Kodak tungsten film.

The reflex camera is used in conjunction with an Ikelite housing. Most photos were taken with a single top mount flash while occasional wide angle subjects were taken with twin strobes. The flash units I use are small in size and output and powered by alkaline batteries. I have found products with nicad power unreliable in remote areas where a constant power source is not always available.

SPECIAL NOTE:

I would welcome correspondence from divers or photographers who might have witnessed unusual behavioural or reproductive activities related to coral reefs or marine animals. Please write to:
Roger Steene
Box 188
Cairns, Qld. 4870
Australia

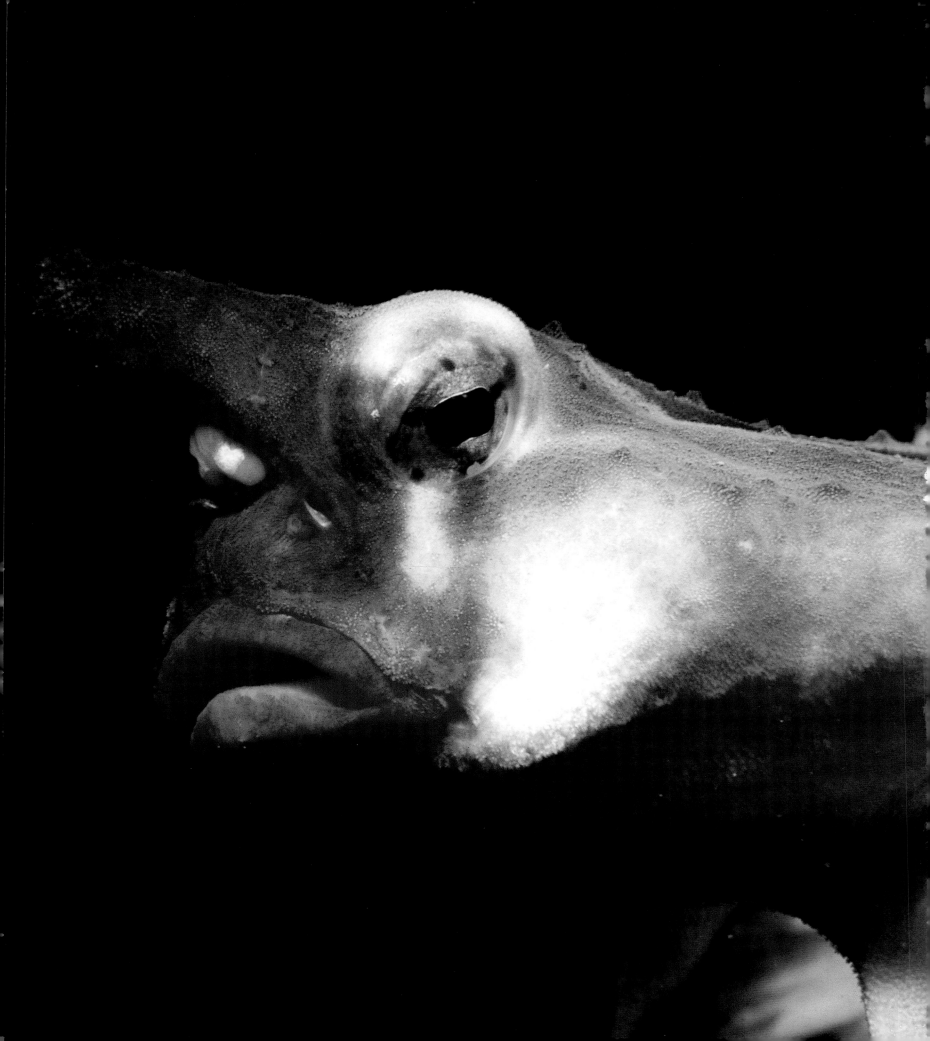